Surviving
IT

ESSENTIAL ADVICE FOR
BUILDING A HAPPY AND HEALTHY
TECHNOLOGY CAREER

PAUL CUNNINGHAM

Published in Australia by Left Brain Publishing
leftbrainpublishing.com.au

Printed in Australia

First Edition

National Library of Australia Cataloguing-in-Publication
entry available for this title at nla.gov.au

ISBN: 978-0-6486612-0-7

Cover and Interior Design: Swish Design

To Hayley, Will, and Abby, thank you for being my support and inspiration every day of this wonderful life we have together.

To my editor and publishing coach Kelly Exeter, thank you for guiding me through the journey of writing this book and getting it into the hands of readers.

To all my friends, mentors, and former colleagues in the IT industry, thank you for everything you have taught me along the way.

For everyone who has shared stories with me, asked questions of me, and those of you who are reading this book right now, I hope that you are able to achieve your own personal idea of the perfect day.

CONTENTS

INTRODUCTION 1

    The perfect day 7

    Remember, this is just the beginning 12

CHAPTER 1: THE INDUSTRY 15

    What working in the IT industry actually looks like 16

    Understanding business 18

    Change is the only constant 23

    New technology, old technology 25

    The technology adoption curve 28

    Chapter 1 Recap 32

CHAPTER 2: FINDING AND LEAVING JOBS 33

    Breaking into the industry 35

    Your resume 37

    Recruiters 46

    Job interviews 52

    Salary negotiations 74

    Starting a new job 84

    Dealing with the 'new job slump' 90

    Stay or go 92

    How to quit a job 94

    How to handle losing a job 107

    Chapter 2 Recap 120

CHAPTER 3: THE BUSINESS OF YOU **123**

Building your network 124

Moving up the career ladder 134

Upskilling and staying employable 138

Blogging and side projects 144

Social media, forums and communities 147

Personal finances 150

Chapter 3 Recap 154

CHAPTER 4: DEALING WITH PEOPLE **157**

Dealing with managers (especially the bad ones) 158

Being managed 164

Dealing with customers 168

How to ask good questions 173

How to be a good team player 178

Chapter 4 Recap 182

CHAPTER 5: PRODUCTIVITY **185**

Developing a coaching habit 187

Taming email 194

Prioritizing tasks 206

Automation 210

Making peace with incremental progress 214

Dealing with interruptions 216

Multitasking 222

Meetings 223

Chapter 5 Recap 230

CHAPTER 6: PERSONAL HEALTH **233**

Burnout 234

Life-work balance 240

Your physical health 246

The importance of eating right. 249

Exercise 259

Drugs and alcohol 263

Chapter 6 Recap 269

CHAPTER 7: VETERAN ADVICE **271**

How to be wrong 271

Technical debt 273

Addiction to firefighting 276

You're not a magician 277

Success as a barrier to success 279

Comfort is the enemy of progress 282

Don't take things personally 285

Chapter 7 Recap 288

CONCLUSION **291**

INTRODUCTION

It was 2am when I found myself upright in bed, gasping for breath. As the chest pains that woke me started to fade, fear and confusion took over.

I'm only 27 years old. Too young for a heart attack, surely?

"It could be stress," the doctor said to me the next day. "What do you do for work?"

"I'm an IT consultant. I work with computers."

It was the seventh year of my career, and from the outside things looked like they were going well. I worked for one of the biggest IT companies in town. I had a senior job title. And I was making pretty good money. I should have been happy.

But the opposite was true. I was miserable. I sat at my desk every day, completely uninterested in the work in front of me. Weighed down by the feeling that I wasn't achieving anything meaningful, I had to force myself to complete my assigned tasks.

I'd also started to gain weight. Friday afternoon drinks turned into Friday all-night benders. Weekends were spent recovering from hangovers. And each Monday morning I dragged myself back into the office, dreading the week ahead.

The unexplained chest pain incident was a wake up call in both a literal and metaphorical sense. When the doctor suggested stress might be the cause, I thought a good antidote would be to seek opportunities that would get me away from the mundane work I was assigned to on a day-to-day basis.

So, I put my hand up to volunteer for any new work that came up and I joined projects with crazy deadlines; working nights and weekends to get everything finished on time.

But despite a few good projects, I kept finding myself back where I started. Unhappy, unhealthy, and searching for something better.

In the end, I came to realize that burnout was actually the reason for how I was feeling. (So it's unsurprising that adding more projects and more pressure to my plate didn't make me feel better.)

And I'd love to say that a blinding moment of clarity followed this realization. One that led to me having a long, fulfilling and meaningful career in IT.

But the reality is, it took me nearly two years to decide to leave that job. The good thing about doing that particular role is it showed me what kind of work I didn't want to be doing in the IT industry. But I still had no real idea of what I did want to do.

So, what followed was a string of seven job titles with six different companies over eight years. Some of those roles were among the best jobs I've ever had. Some weren't so good. Some of them I moved on from in search of new challenges. And some ended for reasons outside of my control: company mergers, bankruptcy, outsourcing, and the global financial crisis.

Along the way, I worked with a full range of teammates from those who were awesome and remain great friends to this day, to those who were complete slackers. I worked under team leaders and managers who ranged from woefully incompetent, right through to the kind who mentored me and helped me to grow my career. I worked for people who were awesome, and people who were awful.

After more than 18 years in the IT industry:

- I understand what I want to do in my career.

- I know which jobs I'll enjoy, and how to find the right companies, customers, and people to work with.

- I take vacations every year with my family (several of them actually), where we completely unplug from work.

- I have time for hobbies and exercise, side projects, and studying new technologies.

In this book, I'm going to share everything I've learned over the past 18 years in the hope it will take you less time than it took me to find a place where you too can survive in the IT industry, and maybe even thrive too.

One of the biggest challenges for IT professionals is understanding where they fit into the big picture along with how businesses look at technology and IT workers. So, in **Chapter 1**, I'll start by sharing how the IT industry works.

The technology industry is full of opportunities, but they aren't just going to be handed to you. In **Chapter 2**, I'll walk you through how to find a new job, whether it's your first job you're looking for, or your next job. I'll teach you how to showcase the skills that make you stand out from the crowd in a competitive job market. I'll cover resume tips and tricks that will get you through the front door with recruiters and employers.

And I'll share my best interview tips. I'll also talk you through how to leave a job when you decide it's time, as I know this is something many people struggle with.

In **Chapter 3**, we'll get into what I call the Business of You. Once you've found your foothold in the IT industry, how do you expand your network, continue to grow your skills, and build a strong foundation for your ongoing career success? I'll show you how the top professionals in the industry get to where they are, and stay there for the long term.

At its core, IT is a people business, not a technology business. People skills are one of the most important soft skills that you can have. As IT professionals we can't sit in the back room and interact with machines all day long. In **Chapter 4**, you'll learn about dealing with people: customers, co-workers, managers, and more. I'll also help you make sure you're treated as a person and not a resource to be consumed and discarded.

In **Chapter 5**, I'll share with you the productivity tips that allowed me to move through a variety of different IT roles, from support, to projects, to consulting, all while maintaining a high level of output. Learning to manage time, break work down into manageable chunks, prioritize tasks and demonstrate results will turn you into the kind of high performer people want to hire and work with.

In **Chapter 6**, we'll talk about your personal health. I'll share with you the same advice I would give to the younger version of myself who was overweight, miserable and had woken up in the middle of the night with chest pains.

In **Chapter 7**, I'll share with you a series of tips and life lessons that I call my Veteran Advice. These are the short pieces of advice I wish I could go back and give my younger self. Advice that would have made my career, especially the early years, just that little bit less rocky.

Throughout this book, I'll share stories of situations I was either a direct participant in, or that I witnessed first hand. I've changed the names and some of the inconsequential details to protect people's privacy, but each story in this book is based on real events.

Before we get into the meat of this book, however, I have an exercise for you to do.

THE PERFECT DAY

What does your perfect day look like?

That's the question I asked myself a few years ago. The answer I came up with went something like this:

> Wake up around 5am, drink a glass of water, and go downstairs to my home gym. After my workout, head back upstairs and make breakfast for my family. Eat my delicious breakfast burrito, drink my coffee, and read a book on my Kindle or some saved articles from around the web on my iPad.
>
> After breakfast, spend a little time with the kids before they bury themselves in a fun activity or head off to school. Then go and do a few hours of work on the projects I have on. Just before lunch, go through my emails and add things that require following up to my to-do list. Then go and eat while reading my Kindle or watching the end of a basketball game.
>
> After lunch, do a little more focused work, then hit my to-do list items for an hour or so. In the late afternoon, do some exercise with the whole family, like a bike ride, a walk, or playing basketball at the park. Pick up something fresh for dinner, and cook a nice, healthy meal for the family.
>
> After dinner when my wife goes to the gym, I'll drink some tea while I do a little reading, watch some Netflix, take an online guitar lesson, or just play some video games. Get to bed around 9pm for a good night's sleep.

That all sounded pretty good to me. Unfortunately, at the time I asked myself that question, my days were nothing like that. In fact, for a large chunk of my IT career my days looked more like this:

> Wake up tired from a late night, scoff down some cereal, and rush out the door to catch the train into the city. After 30 minutes squished in a peak-hour train carriage, I would walk into my building and sit down at my desk then proceed to work through an endless barrage of other people's priorities.
>
> Lunch consisted of whatever food I could run out, buy and be back at my desk in 20 minutes. I would eat at my desk while continuing to deal with issues that were other people's priorities, not my own. All while pretending I couldn't see my gym bag sitting under my desk. After staying late to deal with yet another of someone else's priorities, I would squeeze into another train for the ride home.
>
> At home we would cook whatever fast, convenient meal we could throw together. Then I'd log in remotely and try to close some overdue tasks before stumbling into bed when I couldn't stay awake any longer.

From what I wrote about my perfect day, it was clear the following things were important to me:

- time with family
- healthy eating

- exercise
- work that I enjoy doing
- control over my time
- fun leisure activities
- a good night's sleep

And it was clear that no one was going to gift me days that had those things in it. From what I could see, there were only two ways to achieve something close to my perfect day:

1. I needed to win the lottery.
2. I needed to stop letting my job consume my entire day.

Given the lottery win was not likely to happen, I set about trying to fix my day job.

The first thing I had to do was leave the job I was in at the time in favor of one that allowed me to work more reasonable hours, so I could spend time with my family, get regular exercise, and take the time to eat healthy.

During work hours, I needed to have more control over how my time was spent so I wasn't constantly reacting to other people's priorities, and could do more of the work that I enjoyed.

In the years after I first envisioned that perfect day, I worked in many different roles that met my ideal to some extent. Some jobs had flexible hours, as long as the work got done. Others had a gym near the office, or lockers and showers in the basement, so I could work out at lunch and ride my bicycle to and from work. Some had clear technology roadmaps with reasonable target dates that didn't require a non-stop 150% effort. Some of them had none of those things, and I didn't stay long before moving on to another job.

Of course, the perfect day is not something you can expect to live every single day of your life given you need to factor in things like kids' activities, maintaining a social life, the weather, and so on.

On the work front, crunch time during projects might involve staying late a few nights here and there. Upgrading systems sometimes means working on a weekend. Critical outages need you to keep working on them until they're fixed.

But it has to be said: those should be exceptions. A company that is constantly running on crunch time, or suffering constant outages due to poorly designed systems is not somewhere you want to work. While some overtime or on call work is a fact of life in IT, a consistent 50+ hour week fighting fires is not something we should accept as the norm.

Ultimately, as you read through this book, you'll get the most benefit from the advice if you have a clear idea of what your own perfect day looks like, because you'll know what you're working towards.

And it's worth stating that your perfect day will look different to mine.

- Perhaps you don't mind a long commute, because it lets you get some reading done.
- Perhaps you prefer to spend your weekends playing video games, hiking in the wilderness, or building your own furniture out of recycled wood.
- Perhaps you want to work hard as a contractor for half the year, so you can travel for the other half.

There is no right or wrong. It's all about what you want. To maximize your career and achieve a happy life-work balance, you need to know what you're striving for.

So, before you go on to Chapter 1, grab a piece of paper or a notebook and spend a few minutes writing out what your perfect day looks like right now.

Once that's done, look for the main themes in your answer, and note them down.

Now, as you continue on with reading this book, keep what you've written above in mind as it will dictate how you put the advice in this book to work.

REMEMBER, THIS IS JUST THE BEGINNING

This book is not intended to be the end of your journey to a better career and life. This is just the beginning. There are many areas this book touches on that are covered in far more detail and depth elsewhere. To include that level of depth in this book would make for an impossible read. In fact, I doubt I would ever be able to finish writing it.

So what I hope you get from this book is a sense of hope, possibility, and confidence that you can take control of your *career* in IT and use it to get where you want to be in life.

After you read this book there will be many more steps for you to take. In a sense, you get to choose your own adventure. If you decide that improving your people skills is your first priority, that's what you'll work on first. Meanwhile, another reader might choose to focus on their technical skills. Another will take their first steps to move to a new city, or improve their health.

To help you along the way I have some resources to share with you at **survivingitbook.com/resources**. There you'll find a list of books, blog posts, and other resources that I think will be useful to you.

You can also go to **survivingitbook.com/subscribe** and sign up to the Surviving IT mailing list to be notified when updates to this book are released, and when new resources are added to the website.

Most of all, I hope you'll get in touch with me and let me know how this book helped you. You can email me at **paul@survivingitbook.com**, or find me on Twitter at **@paulcunningham**.

CHAPTER 1
THE INDUSTRY

Before I worked in the IT industry, I co-owned and managed a coin-operated video game arcade. When I tell people about that part of my job history, they inevitably ask me the same question.

"Did you get to play video games all day?"

The answer is no, I did not get to play video games all day. In fact, I barely played them at all.

Most of my days were spent cleaning, dispensing change, restocking the candy and prize displays, more cleaning, more dispensing of change, repairing faulty games, clearing all manner of objects out of the coin slots, and more cleaning. I also had to do the bookkeeping, banking, payroll and marketing while dealing with any other problems that came up on any given day.

Short story: while the temptation to 'just play games' was always there, there were always other, more important, things to be done first.

What does this have to do with working in IT?

Well, I've had many aspiring young IT pros tell me that what lured them to the industry was the thought that they'd get to play with computers all day. As the 'family tech expert,' they were always tinkering with PC hardware, fixing their parents' computer or building gaming rigs for their cousins. All fun stuff for them. Fun stuff they figured they'd get paid to do if only they worked in IT.

WHAT WORKING IN THE IT INDUSTRY ACTUALLY LOOKS LIKE

Despite the fact that I spent my early years in the IT industry working in help desk and desktop support—an area of the industry where you'd most expect to be spending your days tinkering (playing) with computers—I barely ever touched an actual computer (other than my own) in all that time.

We never got to build computers, or fix broken ones. The vendors did that for us. Instead, we spent our days dealing with other matters: creating accounts, resetting passwords, clearing jammed printers, reinstalling software, resetting more passwords, helping Bob get the margins in his Word document just right, finding Jane's files that had been accidentally moved somewhere, and resetting some more passwords. Boring grunt work.

Why did we do all of that boring grunt work? Because that's what the business needed us to do. We didn't get to tinker with gadgets and deploy servers because we were curious about how they worked. We were there to help the employees of the business do their jobs.

Every now and then something that helped the employees of the business do their jobs was also something new and interesting we could derive personal enjoyment from. But those instances were the exception, not the rule.

I say this not to discourage you from working in the industry. I say it because, in order to extract what you need from the industry (i.e. find a role within the industry that gives you something close to your perfect day), you need to understand how it works, and what the motivations are of the people you're working for.

UNDERSTANDING BUSINESS

Every business you will ever work for uses your job function, either directly or indirectly, to make money. That is to say, you're either:

- Producing revenue directly from your efforts, or

- Your efforts support those people in the business who do produce revenue.

Additionally, everyone in the business you're working for is looking for ways to achieve their personal objectives. Often times, they have more objectives than they can reasonably expect to achieve in a week, month, or year. In a 2016 blog post, Jeffrey Snover, a Technical Fellow at Microsoft and the creator of PowerShell, wrote:

> "The most important thing to understand when dealing with people from Microsoft is this: We all have ten jobs and our only true job is to figure out which nine we can fail at and not get fired." [1]

Now, Microsoft is an extreme case. But in most businesses, people will still be juggling three to four things and deciding which one they can let fail. If you've ever gone to your boss with a 'great idea' and been shot down, it's probably not because your idea is dumb. It's more likely your idea doesn't move your boss closer

---

[1] jsnover.com/blog/2014/11/06/working-with-microsoft

to any of the priorities they're focusing on right now. (If your idea does do this, and they still say no, you're probably not making a clear enough case for it.)

Throughout your long IT career, most of your employers will view your job as a necessary part of their business goal, nothing more. They may tell you what those goals are in the broad sense, but the finer details will seldom be shared. This means there will be times you find yourself missing key information about why a request has been denied or a decision has been made.

Why did the business announce millions of dollars in profits, but reject your request for $10,000 to replace an aging server? It could be as simple as that ten grand already being allocated elsewhere in next year's budget. Spending that ten grand on a server harms the other business goal that lost that money from its budget. Sure, in an emergency they'll come up with the cash. But that's a different situation.

In short, things don't always make sense when you don't have the full story. It's helpful to keep that in mind.

This extends to customers as well, regardless of whether the customer is another company you're selling products and services to, or the internal users you support. Your customers view IT as a means to an end, and that end is whatever their job task happens to be at that time.

If their job is entering numbers into an Excel spreadsheet for a monthly report, then a dodgy old keyboard full of sandwich crumbs is as disruptive to their job as a crashed database is to someone else's job. As much as you would love to be writing code in a new language, building scalable cloud infrastructure, or fighting off foreign hackers, there are times when the proverbial crumbs in the keyboard will be what you need to work on instead. The customer only cares about finishing their spreadsheet.

At this point you might be thinking that there's no fun to be had in IT. You might be contemplating a career in fence painting instead. You're pretty certain no one is going to call you at 3am with a fence painting emergency that a $15m sales deal is hinging on. Plus you get a day off whenever it rains.

While the above might be true, it's also true that no job is going to be fun to go to every single day.

There is plenty of enjoyment to be had in the IT industry. Roles where you get to work on the cutting edge of technology, doing meaningful and fulfilling work, absolutely exist. And they solve real business problems. But you'll need to work hard for them. They won't be served up to you on a plate just because you showed up in the industry and expected great things to happen.

It's also important to note, at this point, that satisfaction doesn't always need to come directly from the day-to-day work you're doing. Even if a job isn't fun to do, it can be very satisfying and rewarding if you feel connected to a higher purpose outside of yourself. As an example, spreadsheets and printers aren't fun for me. But knowing my work helps people grow their small businesses, or keeps their pension payments arriving on time, or ensures the right spare parts are available to keep airplanes maintained ... those things make showing up every day a lot more meaningful to me.

If you can create an environment for yourself where your happiness in the industry doesn't rely solely on what you're working on at any given time, this will stand you in good stead for those times in your career when the ideal job isn't available, and you have to take another role for a period of time.

For now, just remember—you are here to serve the business. If you can't do that, they'll find someone else who can.

The Employee Mindset

Your career may open up future opportunities for management, consulting, or even self-employment. But while you're working as an employee, it's helpful to adopt mindsets that will help you deal with decisions and attitudes that are outside of your control:

» Get to know your employer's or customer's business in as much detail as possible. This will help you understand the business needs that are driving their priorities.

» Accept that your view of things may not encompass the bigger picture.

» Get used to asking this question: "Can you help me understand how this decision was made?" People can get defensive if you challenge their decisions, but are usually happy to explain them to anyone who seems interested.

» While creativity and going 'above and beyond' are desirable qualities in employees, if you're not consistently performing your core duties at a high level, your employer will not be pleased. Maintain a solid foundation of performance and build on that.

CHANGE IS THE ONLY CONSTANT

In my first IT job I worked on a help desk. Because we supported people interstate, my phone was specially coded to make long distance calls. I was not able to make international calls, however, because they were expensive. A single phone call could easily cost hundreds of dollars.

On the same day I am writing this chapter, I had a three-way video conference call from my home in Australia with two other people in Chicago and Salt Lake City. We could all see and hear each other in high definition, and share our screens with each other when we needed to show something on our computers. We spoke for nearly an hour. The entire call cost me nothing, and cost them a few dollars a month for the service they use.

Technology moves fast. The technology you work with at the beginning of your career may not exist by the time you finish your career. This is both a good and bad thing for IT professionals.

If you ask an IT professional what they like about their job, they'll often tell you they enjoy the constant exposure to new technology and the excitement of learning new things every day.

But if you listen to two IT professionals talking to each other about their jobs, you'll often hear them complain about how the new thing is not as good as the old thing. They'll reminisce about the old thing and all the ways that it was good. They'll say if it were up to them they'd have chosen a different new thing to replace the old thing, not the one they ended up with.

Why do those two different conversations take place? The reasons are fairly simple. Despite the impression that technology workers are somehow different to other people, we're still human. Like everyone else, when we find something that we understand and are good at doing, we get comfortable. Change disrupts that comfort by introducing new things that we don't understand yet. So we go back to being uncomfortable again.

Some people enjoy that process. They thrive on the discomfort of not understanding new technology. Seeking knowledge is exciting for them. At different times in your career you'll enjoy that feeling too. Many people switch between being someone who enjoys comfort, and someone who enjoys discomfort, depending on the situation.

How do we deal with constant and, at times unwelcome, change? Do we need to become expert industry analysts, able to predict which emerging trends will break through and achieve widespread adoption?

No, not at all. For one thing, nobody can accurately predict where the IT industry will go 100% of the time. But more importantly, it's exhausting to try. Your energy is better spent dealing with the challenges that are in your path today.

I, personally, work to a simple mantra: Expect nothing, and accept everything.

NEW TECHNOLOGY, OLD TECHNOLOGY

When I entered the industry, a business ran on a collection of servers in a room. That room was usually within sight of the IT team whose job it was to keep the servers running. My desk was about ten paces from the server room door at the first customer site I worked on. Each server took up space on a bench or in a rack. And the server team, the ones who knew the hardware intimately, were always busy. When they weren't installing new servers, they were fixing broken ones, or removing old ones. There was always something for them to do.

One day, a new technology called virtualization came along. With virtualization, we could run multiple 'virtual machines' (VMs) on one powerful server, instead of running lots of less powerful servers. At first, virtualization was slow and cumbersome to use. But it got better, and virtualization became the first choice of customers looking for maximum efficiency and return on investment (ROI).

Suddenly, the server team had fewer servers to deal with. With fewer servers there was less work for them to do. Those who were willing to learn about the new virtualization technology were retrained into new roles. Those who were not, found themselves out on the street looking for a new job that needed their skills.

Some years later, we started to hear about this new idea of cloud computing. With cloud computing, you could run your VMs in big data centers hosted by Microsoft or Amazon. This meant you didn't need to deal with the big, powerful virtualization hosts yourself. Again, at first it was slow and cumbersome to use. There were concerns about performance, security, and costs. But as the cloud matured, those concerns were largely solved, and customers began moving their servers to the cloud.

Suddenly, the virtualization team had fewer servers to manage. Maybe even none at all, if their employer went fully to the cloud. Those who were willing to learn about the new cloud services were retrained into new roles. Those who were not, found themselves out on the street.

This pattern of new technology becoming old technology exists across the entire industry. Whether you're a server engineer, a software developer, a database analyst, or a security expert, the industry is going to keep moving along like an ocean current.

If you want to swim against the current, in the long term you're going to find it hard to keep your career alive. Those server engineers who ignored virtualization turned out to be wrong, even if it took several years before their lack of virtualization skills really started to hurt their career.

That's not to say you need to jump on every new trend. It's possible to make a wrong bet and end up in the wrong place skills wise. The key is to work out where you typically sit on the technology adoption curve. Then you need to figure out the risks of moving one way or another (if at all) on that curve.

THE TECHNOLOGY ADOPTION CURVE

Technology moves through a predictable adoption life cycle. Where you stand on that life cycle influences your career opportunities and your job security. It also influences your happiness. If you have a desire to work with the latest products, then you'll be unhappy working at a company that is a late adopter of new technology. If you hate change, you won't enjoy working at the cutting edge.

Adoption of new technologies falls into these categories:

- Innovators
- Early adopters
- Early majority
- Late majority
- Laggards

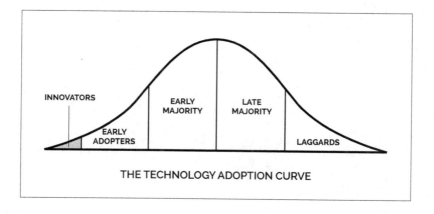

THE TECHNOLOGY ADOPTION CURVE

The categories were described by Everett M. Rogers, an assistant professor of rural sociology at Ohio State University, in his 1962 publication titled Diffusion of Innovations.

Innovators go first, and take on a lot of risk in the process. But they get the highest reward for that risk. Many pioneers and thought leaders are playing in this space. In return for their risk they gain access to opportunities for high-priced consulting and product management roles.

Early adopters go second. These tend to be community leaders who are able to translate the work of innovators into practical applications. Many trainers and authors operate in this space because being the first to get a book or training course to market provides the best return. Early adopters can make a name for themselves by being first. This leads to a consistent stream of employment, speaking and consulting opportunities. It can also mean a disrupted lifestyle (e.g. a lot of travel), and high churn rate as they move from job to job chasing the newest technologies.

The **early majority** show up when a technology has proven that it is viable for widespread adoption. They are able to learn from the teachings of early adopters, and apply those teachings to their own situations. A lot of standards and best practices are cemented during this phase. They tend to have stable job prospects and the ability to move on to new roles when they want to.

The **late majority** adopt technologies that are mature and stabilized. The late majority is willing to forgo the latest features and benefits in return for the lower perception of risk. The reality may be that they miss out on the best performance, security, and value on offer. They are most at risk of losing jobs to outsourcing and offshoring, due to the lower perceived value of their skills.

Laggards come last. Laggards come in many forms, and it's not always a bad thing to operate in this space. In my hometown, there was a time when the last few Novell GroupWise admins could command very high contract rates. There were only a few customers in town, and the supply/demand ratio favored the experts. But these opportunities don't last forever. Laggards run the risk of their skills falling out of date and having no market value at all.

Throughout your career you can move through different parts of the technology life cycle. It will depend on your geographic area, your personal circumstances (e.g. health, age, family), and your natural abilities. A person close to retirement age might be quite happy to run out their final years as a laggard. A younger person with decades of work ahead of them should be trying to move towards the front half of the cycle.

That doesn't mean everyone should strive to be an innovator. One person will enjoy staying up all night, testing and breaking things in order to work out groundbreaking uses for technology. Another person will prefer to do their 9-5, read books in the evening, and go fishing on weekends. Neither is right or wrong. As long as you're happy and you understand how your personal lifestyle integrates with your work, you can have a successful career.

Also keep in mind that when you're hearing the most marketing noise about something, that product is in the early adopter to early majority phase. It's worth remembering that where the most marketing is happening doesn't always reflect the most in-demand jobs for your market. Focus on what makes you happy and employable in your area, not the Next Big Thing that is years away from reaching your market.

CHAPTER 1 RECAP

- Working in the IT industry may not involve getting to 'play with computers' all day, but that doesn't mean there isn't fun to be had.

- If you understand how business works, and where your role sits in the ecosystem of the business you are working for, you will experience less frustration with decisions you may not understand.

- Sometimes, you might need to find your fun outside of work hours in order to ride out a job that you need badly, but doesn't stimulate you.

- Change is a part of every industry, not just the IT industry. Accepting change as a constant and being able to embrace change with a good attitude will make you a desirable employee.

- Figuring out where you sit on the technology adoption curve will help you make good decisions about the right employer for you. (Something I'll touch on more in the next chapter).

CHAPTER 2
FINDING AND LEAVING JOBS

After my video game business closed, I looked around for what to do next. I thought the 'Information Technology' industry looked interesting. So I enrolled in a course, studied as hard as I could, and landed my first job a year later.

Okay. That all sounds very easy. The reality was much more difficult.

The course I chose was the easiest one available—hardware maintenance. (Basically I trained to become a PC repair technician.) It also seemed like the closest thing to my previous work in the video game business. I reasoned that if I could fix a pinball machine, I could fix a PC.

The first job offer I got was a glorified courier position. It involved driving around town picking up dead monitors and returning them to base for repair. "Do that for six to twelve months," the interviewer told me, "and you could move up to a PC technician role."

The salary offered was incredibly low so I declined.

Unfortunately, it took another two months to receive my next job offer for a help desk position. I gladly accepted the role, one because it was closer to what I wanted to be doing, but two, because I was in a pretty dire financial position at that point.

Not only was I in debt from the training course, I'd also moved from my home town up to the city to improve my job prospects. On the first day of work I had to borrow bus money just to get there. My lunch was a small tin of tuna, and nothing else. I begged the payroll department to do a partial pay run for me for that first week so I didn't need to wait a full two weeks to see my first pay. When the check came via internal mail I sprinted to the bank down the street to deposit it just before they closed. I paid back the borrowed bus fare, and was able to have some bread with my can of tuna the next day.

In hindsight, I could have chosen a more difficult course and become a programmer. The demand for programmers was sky high at the time thanks to the Y2K bug. Programmers were graduating from the same training institute where I studied hardware maintenance and were landing jobs immediately. Maybe if I'd become a developer in 1999 I'd be living in Silicon Valley today making megabucks at Google or Facebook?

But the reality was, I was flat broke at the time and going into debt to fund my training. The shorter and cheaper hardware maintenance course was all I felt comfortable with.

BREAKING INTO THE INDUSTRY

If you're trying to break into the industry today, here are some lessons you can take from my experience.

1. Know your market

I can list off a bunch of technologies here that you should learn today. But, that isn't going to be useful if nobody in your area is hiring people with those skills. Before you commit to a learning path, do your research to see what job opportunities exist where you live. Look at the advertised positions to see what they list as required and desired skills. Use those as a guide to determine where you should focus your education.

I chose hardware maintenance without doing any real research. Near the end of my training I attended an industry breakfast and sat next to two recruiters, neither of whom were hiring people with my skills.

They wanted programmers. The breakfast yielded me no job interviews. Live and learn!

2. Get out and meet people

Go to meetups in your area and introduce yourself to people who already work in the industry. Ask them what they look for when they hire for entry level roles. Meeting people in person is best, but online contacts are also useful. I didn't have the convenience of Facebook, LinkedIn or any of the other online technical communities that exist today, and I lived in a relatively small town away from where the jobs were. I couldn't afford the petrol to drive my car up to the city for any industry meetups or events, so I just had to keep applying for jobs cold.

3. Get online and become known

These days it's easier than ever to create an online presence and earn a good reputation that makes people want to hire you. You don't need to be employed to share your knowledge. Help your fellow beginners with their problems. Be open and public, and keep your reputation clean (don't get into fights online, nobody wins). You don't need to be famous around the world. All it takes is a few people in your community who recognize your abilities and know you're looking for a career.

4. Be open to accepting less than ideal jobs

When you're employed, it's easier to find your next job than it was to find your first job. You'll be getting paid and growing your network, and you'll be under less pressure to take just any job you're offered. That very first job I turned down, even though it was low paying, it would have at least helped me move to the city and kept me from sinking further into debt. In turning it down, I also turned down the opportunity to travel to lots of customer sites and meet people who I could strike up a conversation with, and ask for advice. I'm fortunate it worked out okay in the end, but it was an opportunity I should have taken.

YOUR RESUME

If you're going to be applying for jobs, you're going to need a resume. Before putting one together, it's important to remember this: the sole purpose of your resume is to get you an interview. Your resume pitches your suitability for the job. It's a sales pitch, and it should be the simplest one you've ever made, because the buyer (the company advertising the job) is telling you exactly what they want to buy.

If you have one resume that you send to every potential employer, you're doing it wrong. Generic resumes almost always miss the target by a wide margin. Prospective employers are only tangentially interested in the full range of your skills and experience. What they really want to know, and quickly, is how well you match up with their specific requirements.

If you're dealing with a recruiter, they will ask for a general resume to keep on file and match you with opportunities. But they should also be asking you for tailored resumes for specific roles. If not, ask them if there's a way you can provide them with tailored resumes. If you leave it up to them they'll make edits to your resume themselves, which can lead to some awkward moments during interviews if the recruiter has added something to your resume that isn't true.

A good resume says everything it needs to say in as few words as possible. For most IT professionals a resume only needs to be one to two pages long, with all of the most important information contained on the first page. Recruiters and employers make a decision about your resume in 10-30 seconds at most. If you don't grab their attention in that time, you can easily be overlooked.

So how do you ensure you grab their attention? You write your resume to match the requirements of the job. If the job ad is for a server administrator with VMware, Windows Server and Microsoft SQL Server skills, you must clearly show your experience in those areas right up front on the first page of your resume. Don't oversell or undersell your experience. Everything on your resume must be defensible if you make it to a job interview.

A few lines stating your suitability for the role could say:

> Server administrator with over 5 years' experience in VMware infrastructure management, Windows Server (2008 to 2016) administration, and Microsoft SQL Server support.

That statement makes no claim to have *designed* VMware infrastructure, and in an interview is easily defensible by explaining that you were administering an existing environment that was already deployed. If the employer is looking for some design or deployment experience, you can sell your experience as having taught you the merits of a particular design model, any flaws you noticed, how you would avoid them in future, and what else you've learned through additional training and certification (if that is true). This shows employers you are able to learn from other people's work, can gain an understanding of environments you didn't personally deploy, and are not tied to a single way of doing things.

Next, list your current and previous roles in reverse chronological order. For each role, briefly describe the industry or business they were in, the size of the environment, your responsibilities, and any projects that are relevant to the job you're applying for. Only list projects you were personally involved in. (Don't list projects that happened to occur while you were there, but didn't involve you in any way.) Again, you need to highlight the specific skills the job is asking for.

As you get further back in your employment history, you can start to reduce the amount of detail in each role, particularly as the roles become less relevant to the job you're applying for. After 20 years in the industry, my first five years, all of which were at the same company, are summarized as 'various roles' and don't include any projects. If my more recent experience isn't enough to get me the job, there's no chance the work I did in the '90s will make a difference.

Don't take job ads too literally though. Many job ads ask for more skills and experience than they'll actually be able to get. If a company wants a Senior Systems Engineer with Exchange, SQL, XenDesktop, NetScaler, Barracuda, Azure, and Docker experience, that's a lot to expect. Outside of a total economic disaster like the global financial crisis of 2007-2009, employers are usually desperate for good quality employees. While they might get lucky and find someone with all the skills they want, it's much more likely they'll accept someone with fewer of those skills, so long as that person can show other desirable qualities.

Good examples of 'other desirable qualities' are soft skills and side projects. Technical skills can be taught and trained. Soft skills are developed over time, and are more valuable.

Communication is one notable soft skill that can overcome a deficiency in technical skills. The quality of your resume alone will indicate whether you are a good communicator. Spelling and grammar errors in a resume will send it straight to the reject pile, so make sure you've thoroughly proofread it. If you have any online content such as a blog or YouTube channel, that will also demonstrate your communication skills.

Side projects demonstrate soft skills such as persistence, time management, project management, attention to detail, and commitment to quality. They can also demonstrate to a prospective employer that you write clean code, handle feedback and bug reports well, and make logical decisions about how to build and share your project with others.

Educational qualifications should also be included. How much emphasis you place on your education depends on the role. A graduate or junior role might require a heavy emphasis on your grades and the school you went to. After a few years, however, it is only relevant that you graduated. Whether you got an A or a B in high school English is not as important. Later in your career as you get into more senior roles, education can swing back into the spotlight as employers look for things like masters' degrees or specialist qualifications. Let the job ad guide you as to the level of detail they're looking for.

The same applies to technical certifications. If they ask for it, you should list it. If you have others that are closely relevant, list those as well. But don't oversell the 20+ hardware and networking certifications you've done that have no relevance to the job. By all means list them in an 'additional qualifications' section of your resume, but don't waste prime front page real estate on them. Relevance is more important than quantity.

Many employers treat education as a box-ticking exercise for job applicants, rather than an integral part of the job itself. In Chapter 3 we'll discuss upskilling and staying employable, and the role that certifications play in that process. Certifications and other education are important, but later in your career it is good experience that wins over paper qualifications.

Don't be shy about including a few personal interests at the end of your resume. Employers do like to see that you are human and have a life outside of work, and that you will have things in common with other employees. Personal interests are also good conversation items in interviews and can help you to establish rapport with the interviewers.

Your resume should also include referees who can vouch for your skills and experience. When you're applying for new jobs it can be awkward to get referees from your current job, especially if you feel you need to get a reference from someone you report to directly. Asking your manager if they can be included as a reference is obviously a signal that you're looking elsewhere, and may trigger a conversation you're not ready to have.

You can also ask others in your team to be referees. For example, if you are a junior developer, you can ask a senior developer you've worked closely with to be a referee. After all, they can often provide a better view of your abilities than a manager who is less involved in your day-to-day work. You can also ask other people that you've worked with, such as project managers. It's also always worth maintaining some good contacts at previous jobs you've left on good terms who can be a referee for you in future.

If someone agrees to be your referee, it's important that you let them know you will be providing their details to potential employers. Obviously you want them to be prepared to answer a phone call or email and discuss your suitability for a role. Planting that seed early helps them turn their mind to what they might say about you. To be considerate of your referees' privacy, you can submit resumes to prospective employers with the names of your referees and where you worked with them, and then add 'contact details available on request.' If you make it to the interview stage you can provide another copy of your resume that has the full details, and then let your referees know you made it to the interview stage and that they might receive a call from the company you applied to.

Writing Resumes

Remembering the sole purpose of a resume is to get you a job interview, here are some tips for crafting a great resume:

» Always tailor your resume to the requirements of the job you're applying for.

» Use a professional email address, such as Gmail, Outlook.com, or your own domain name if you have one. john@johnsmith.io is okay, especially if you also have a blog or portfolio site on that domain. john@420blazeclan.info might give the wrong impression.

» List technical skills that are relevant to the role, but don't waste space on excessive detail. Writing 'Windows Server 2008 and later' is enough information. You don't need to list every individual version of Windows you've ever touched.

» Describe what you did in your employment history, not what your team did. If you were a member of the 'server management team,' explain your personal responsibilities in that team and the projects you participated in.

» Don't list skills you can't defend in an interview. You are not skilled in 'PowerShell scripting' if you've only copied code from someone else's GitHub or blog post and run it.

» Proofread your resume more than once. Read it to yourself out loud. If you're not confident in your writing abilities, ask a friend to read it for you.

» Don't hold back from applying for jobs just because you think you don't tick every box on the job ad. You miss 100% of the shots you don't take.

RECRUITERS

If you're in the market for a new job, you're eventually going to deal with a recruiter. Employers like to use recruiters because it shields them from the messy part of the hiring process. Recruiters handle time-consuming activities like sifting through hundreds of applicants and doing basic personality checks. They can also provide payroll and contract services.

As a job seeker, it's important to remember that no matter what a recruiter says to you, ultimately they work for the employer. Filling the employer's vacancy is their objective. To that end, recruiters are looking for a skilled, competent professional with good personal skills who is available in as short a time period as possible.

Submitting your resume to a recruiter

When dealing with a recruiter, your resume fulfills a different function compared to when you're applying for a job vacancy.

- For a job vacancy, the goal of your resume is to get you an interview.
- When you are going through a recruiter, the goal of your resume is to get you through whatever filters they have set up to match candidates to vacancies.

Fortunately, the same resume you tailor for a specific job ad should also tick the boxes the recruiter is looking for in their candidate matches. The main difference is that instead of getting you an interview with the employer, the resume gets you a screening interview with the recruiter.

Interviewing with a recruiter

During a screening interview the recruiter is trying to answer two questions:

1. Is this candidate suitable for this role?
2. Will this candidate embarrass me if I send them for an interview?

I've seen job seekers treat the recruiter interview as an annoying obstacle to their goal of landing a job. The problem there is, if you put anything but your best foot forward with the recruiter, you're not going to get any further with that job opportunity. You need to present yourself the way you would to an employer. Even if the recruiter invites you to coffee, treat it like your one shot at getting the job:

- dress nicely
- listen intently
- show interest in what they're saying

- be confident in your answers
- be honest about your skills and experience and
- ask good questions about the job opportunity.

What about those recruiter interviews that happen on short notice? I received one such invitation for coffee and had to show up without my normal interview attire of suit and tie. The first time it happened I didn't say anything about it and the interview ended on an awkward note when the recruiter asked me if I owned a suit to wear to the interview with the employer. The next time it happened I simply mentioned up front that I had no issues dressing more nicely for an interview, but that I was dressed more comfortably that day for some equipment moves we were doing.

How recruiters make their money

Recruiters are compensated for successfully placing candidates in roles. They either earn a one-time commission for filling a permanent role, or they earn a commission on top of a contractor's hourly or daily rate.

Many recruitment agencies also provide contractor services.

If you've never worked as a contractor before, you may not realize that in order to get paid by your employer, you will need a company structure and some form of insurance to protect you from professional and public liability. You can either go to the trouble of setting up your own company for this purpose, or you can use your recruitment company's contractor services.

These generally include payroll services and professional insurance cover. The fees for these services would be deducted from your hourly or daily rate. Let's say your recruitment company negotiates an hourly rate of $70 per hour with your employer. $60 per hour will go to you and $10 per hour will go to the recruitment company to cover payroll services and insurance.

That might seem like an outrageous overhead. Why should the recruitment company get so much money for processing your timesheet and payroll? This way of thinking misses the most important point in negotiating your compensation: it doesn't really matter what the recruitment company is making from the deal, as long as you get what you want. Are you happy with $60 per hour? If not, negotiate for more. Most recruiters will have some wiggle room, and the worst that can happen is they say no. If you're not getting the rate you want from this contract, seek better rates on your next one. Over a few years of contracting it's not unheard of to boost your rate by a few dollars per hour each time you land a new role. (I'll discuss salary negotiations in more detail later in this chapter.)

The final word on recruiters

The important thing to remember here is that if you work primarily as a contractor, understanding how the recruitment industry works and building relationships with recruiters is crucial. They keep detailed databases of candidates' skills and experience, as well as personalities. If they already know you're a good candidate from previous interactions, they're more likely to call you first when new opportunities come up. The more money they're making from placing you in roles, the happier they are. For that reason I've always been happy to take a few minutes and speak to recruiters when they call. Even when I'm not actively job seeking I hear them out because you never know what golden opportunities might come your way if you keep an open mind. Most of the time we have a pleasant chat, they update their database with my current status, and I say it's fine if they want to check back with me again in a few months.

Dealing With Recruiters

Since recruiters are an unavoidable fact of life when it comes to job seeking, here are some tips for maximizing your relationship with them:

» Remember the recruiter's job is finding the right candidate for the employer's needs, not finding you your dream job.

» Tailor your resume for applications to recruiters just as you would any other advertised job.

» Treat recruiter screening interviews as you would any other job interview. They are judging if you're suitable to be sent to an employer.

» Practice stating your career and skills summary, especially your current role, so that you can reel it off quickly and easily if a recruiter calls.

» Always take recruiters' calls. If they're updating their database, give them any new information that will help them match you to current or future roles.

JOB INTERVIEWS

Some people are perfectly comfortable in job interviews, and some people are terrified of them. There's no shame in being nervous about an interview. Sitting in front of strangers and answering questions is difficult, especially if you're not used to doing it.

The first thing to know about job interviews is that you'll get better at them the more times you do them. When I was first trying to get into the IT industry I sat through dozens of job interviews. The first few were a little shaky, but I got through them okay. After that it became quite easy. Practice makes perfect, right?

So here's tip number one for you if you are actively seeking a new job: go to as many job interviews as you can. There's no rule that says you have to accept a job after you've been interviewed. I'm not suggesting you waste an employer's time by sitting a bunch of practice interviews you have no intention of following through on, but if an opportunity shows even a hint of promise, and you get to the stage where you're invited to interview, by all means go and do the interview.

When you're invited to an interview there are a few pieces of crucial information that you need. Often these will be provided to you, but if anything is missing you should ask. Make sure you get all these written down or provided in an email so you don't make a mistake and show up on the wrong day or to the wrong location.

- **What is the time and date of the interview?** You'd be surprised how many people screw this one up.

- **What is the exact location of the interview?** Ask where you need to report to, e.g. building security, or reception on a specific floor. If you're unfamiliar with the location ask about parking options, or the best public transport to use.

- **Who will you be interviewing with?** I like to at least know their job titles, but the names are also useful as it gives you the opportunity to try and memorize the names beforehand.

- **Who should you call if there are any problems?** Life happens, and if you're sick or stuck in traffic you need to be able to let the interviewer know.

- **What should you wear?** This question is best asked of a recruiter, but if you have to ask the prospective employer directly, try and find a good way to spin the question. The weather is hot most of the year where I live, so I would say something like, "It's been pretty warm this week so if you don't mind me asking does your interview panel expect full suit and tie for candidates or is just a jacket okay?"

The general rule for what to wear is that you should dress one level above what the company will expect you to wear on the job. If they're a casual 'jeans and t-shirts' place, then nice pants with a collared shirt and coat or business jacket should be fine. If they wear business shirts and trousers, upgrade your look to a full suit and tie. If you're unsure, just ask them (or ask your recruiter). Or if you're afraid to ask, go scope out the place beforehand and see what employees wear as they arrive at work.

You should also take into account the 'prestige' of the place. Top-tier employers might allow a casual dress code for their staff, but expect something much more from interview candidates. If in doubt, it's better to be overdressed than underdressed. If there's a comfort issue, the interviewer will probably let you downgrade a little anyway. I once sat down in full suit and tie in a room that was pretty warm, and everyone else was just wearing business shirts with sleeves rolled up. When I realized I was going to start sweating I simply asked them if they'd mind if I took off my jacket to be more comfortable.

Whatever you wear, make it presentable. Wrinkled and stained won't get you the job. If you're expecting to interview to a lot of places, invest in a nice set of 'interview clothes' that you know will look nice every time you wear them. They don't need to be expensive. You might be surprised by how much of a difference clean clothes that fit properly can make in your appearance.

When I finished my IT training back in 1998 I started interviewing during spring and into summer. It's hot most of the year where I live, but that summer was particularly hot. I owned a beat up old car with barely-working air-conditioning, and I was applying for jobs in a city that was an hour from home. After showing up to my first interview in a sweaty and wrinkled business shirt I had to change my strategy. I wore a t-shirt for the drive and left home early enough to find the interview location. (Keep in mind this was back in the days of no GPS navigation systems. I didn't have Google Maps guiding me to my destination and choosing the optimal route through traffic. I had to find my way using an old school street map and just hope for the best.)

Once I found the place I was interviewing at, I would scope out the parking situation, then drive a short distance away and find somewhere free to park so I could get out of my car and cool down. At the right moment I would change into my business shirt and tie, drive or walk the short distance to the interview, and arrive fresh and presentable.

Later in my career I used a similar strategy if I were ducking out for an interview during the work day. I'd find a nearby location to chill out and cool down, then head to the interview looking calm and professional. If the building you're interviewing in has a public lobby just head there, or to the lobby of a neighboring building.

If you're interviewing somewhere more suburban just look for a McDonald's or a coffee shop where you can stop and chill out. If your staging location has restrooms that's also ideal, allowing you to wash your hands and face, fix your hair, straighten your tie, and use the restroom before you go to your interview.

Staging yourself nearby for a few minutes also helps you to arrive at the optimal time for your interview. No employer wants candidates to arrive too early. It creates an awkward situation where they have to deliberately leave you waiting for a long time before the scheduled interview takes place. Nor should you arrive right on the time of your appointment. If the employer is running back to back interviews they will be trying to stick to a schedule, and you arriving right on time will eat into your actual interview time. It's best to arrive five to ten minutes before your interview. If you're asked to report to security on the ground floor, allow a few extra minutes for someone to come down in the elevators to get you. If you're reporting directly to a reception area on their floor, five to ten minutes is enough.

If you're running late, call ahead to let them know. Ideally you'd have a good reason for this: traffic problems, parking problems, or just caught up in a work situation that you couldn't get away from. I have run late for interviews myself and still got the job. Most employers will understand, and if they don't then it might be a sign they're a bit inflexible with how life sometimes gets in the way of work.

If you need to use a restroom before your interview, find one before you report to reception. Or if you're not sure where they are, let the receptionist know that you're here for an interview but ask if you can use their restrooms before they notify the person you're supposed to meet. It's a bit awkward if the first interaction with your interviewer is to ask them where the restrooms are, or if you have to exit the restrooms and come face to face with them waiting for you (I hope you washed your hands!).

For some employers the interview begins the second you show up at the location. Some employers will scrutinize every single thing you do after you arrive. Were you polite to the reception staff? Did you sit or stand in the waiting area? Did you read a magazine, and if so, which one? Personally, I like to just stand in the waiting area. If they have a nice view out the window, as many companies do, I just look out the window and compose my thoughts. No fidgeting, whistling or playing with my phone.

You'll be collected from the waiting area by someone who is escorting you to the interview room, or by one of the interviewers. Either way, try to learn their name. When it's just the person escorting candidates it still gives a good impression when you're able to thank them by name after they show you into the interview room.

Most interviews will be conducted by more than one person, giving you two or three names to learn quickly. I'm terrible with names. It's just one of my weaknesses. If you introduced me to a room of people I'd be lucky to remember a single name. So I try to use those little tricks that we're taught, like looking them directly in the eye and repeating the person's name back to them immediately, "Nice to meet you, Jane."

Once the interview has started just get comfortable and breathe while they begin their questions. Some nervousness or excitement is normal for the first few minutes of an interview. Just focus on your breathing and concentrate on what the interviewers are saying. Don't reach for the glass of water in front of you, your hands will probably shake. Save it for when you are feeling more comfortable and confident in the interview.

How to answer common interview questions

Good interviewers will give you a brief rundown of the company and the position they are hiring for. But some like to go straight for the tricky questions. You should prepare for the most common questions interviewers open with:

"Tell us about yourself ..."

This is the question so many people fear, but should be the easiest to answer. After all, you are the world's expert on yourself. Nobody knows more about you than you do. This is your chance to tell your story in a concise and interesting way. Here's the type of answer I usually give.

> "Well, most recently I've been working as a JOB TITLE at COMPANY. My team is responsible for OUR GENERAL AREA and within the team I am the lead on MY SPECIALTIES. Before that I worked for a variety of companies as a consultant or internal IT ops member, mostly working on SOMETHING RELEVANT TO THE JOB I'M INTERVIEWING FOR. I've been working here in Brisbane for almost 20 years now after I moved here from the Gold Coast to get into the industry. Outside of work I enjoy spending time with my family and A FEW HOBBIES OF MINE. We've been planning our holiday for the end of the year so we're all pretty excited about that at the moment."

Keep it short and to the point. Don't waffle on about yourself. Treat it like an elevator pitch. You want to convey a few relevant facts about yourself that get them interested in learning more about you, and also show that you can confidently speak about yourself.

"What do you know about our company?"

They want to know that you've done at least a little research about the company. Try not to just rattle off basic information from their web page. If they've recently been in the news, or are well known for a major product or project, talk about that and why it interests you. If you've heard of them through friends in the industry, talk about what you've heard and why that makes you interested in working for them.

"What made you want to apply for this job?"

Even if your reason is 'for the money,' come prepared with another reason. Telling them that you're underpaid now will hurt your salary negotiations later. Good answers include things like looking for new challenges, opportunity to work more with a technology that the new role focuses on, opportunity to change industries, relocation for personal reasons, and so on.

"Tell us about a time that you …"

These types of questions are easier to answer if you remember that everyone loves a good story. Having some anecdotes about your past work helps to demonstrate the depth of experience you have with different products. Keep them short and to the point, and don't try too hard to make them funny. Employers are really interested in the experience you've gained, not whether you've been in a bunch of hilarious situations over the years.

"What would you say are your strengths and weaknesses?"

This is kind of a trick question. A candidate I was interviewing once answered that his biggest weakness was that he couldn't handle stressful situations, and his mind just seemed to shut down when under pressure. While I appreciated his honesty, that was definitely not the right answer. But it's also not a good look to sit there and brag about how you're 100% strengths and 0% weaknesses. Nobody is perfect and you'll just come across as arrogant. By all means talk up your strengths. This is the time to do it. But you must demonstrate some self-awareness by talking about weaknesses as well.

My approach to the 'strengths and weaknesses' question is to talk about something I've struggled with in the past, and the techniques I've developed to overcome it. For example, I would mention that early in my career I was guilty of spending too long working on a problem that was beyond my skills before I would seek help from others. That's an obvious weakness because it delays resolution for the problem and makes me seem like someone who doesn't work well in a team. But I would then explain how I was able to overcome that weakness by setting a time limit for myself before I had to ask a colleague for help. I'd also share that before I go to my colleague, I spend a few minutes preparing my explanation of the problem. That serves two purposes. The first is that in preparing the explanation in my mind, or on paper, I often stumble across the answer myself anyway. The second purpose is that it ensures I have all the relevant information about the problem ready, so I don't waste my colleague's time.

By explaining how I've overcome weaknesses in the past I demonstrate self-awareness and an ability to find workarounds and solutions to my personal flaws.

Technical questions

Interviews for technical roles will include technical questions. There should be no surprises here. The interviewers are going to ask you technical questions about the products they listed on the job ad. They're also going to ask you technical questions about the skills you claim to have on your resume. You should go into the interview prepared to answer these. That might mean you need to brush up on some terminology you haven't dealt with recently. You should also check to see if anything has changed between the version of a product you're already familiar with, and the version the job position requires. Even if you haven't used V2 of a product, being able to demonstrate you're aware of what's changed since V1 is a good thing.

As your interview moves from the common opening questions I've detailed in the section above, to technical questions, you need to keep your wits about you. Many candidates I've interviewed have done themselves a disservice by jumping into the answer as soon as the question is asked. I've often had people start answering in a way that is completely off from where the question was actually intended to take the conversation. In their rush to show how smart they are, candidates have ended up giving some shockingly wrong answers.

Learn from their mistakes. Instead of launching straight into your answer, take a moment to consider what you've just been asked. You can pause for a few breaths before you start answering. It's perfectly okay to do this, and shows that you take a calm approach to problems.

If you're not sure what they want to hear, try to ask a clarifying question before you answer. If you were asked about how you would handle a particular scenario, ask a few questions to establish some assumptions about the situation before you proceed with the answer. That can make the original question clearer and will ensure that your answer is closely aligned to what the interviewers want to hear about.

Avoid one word answers, even if the question can be answered with a simple yes or no. If you're asked "Have you ever worked with Product X?" don't answer "Yes." Instead answer "Yes, I was responsible for managing Product X at the last company I worked at. It was used to achieve X, Y and Z for the business."

If you flat out don't know the answer to a question, or don't understand it, say so. Don't try to guess or lie your way through the situation. In one of my earliest interviews I was asked if I was comfortable working with relational databases. I didn't have the slightest clue at the time what a relational database was but said "Yes," anyway. I'm 100% sure the interviewer knew I was lying. And I didn't get that job.

Much later in my career I was asked during an interview how I would approach a particular problem with a Citrix environment. I answered that I had no hands-on experience with Citrix environments (which was true), and didn't understand the scenario they were describing other than it sounded bad for the users. Instead I offered to explain how I would approach a problem with a product I was completely unfamiliar with. The interview panel was fine with that, and we spent a few minutes on that topic before moving on. They later offered me the job, so it obviously wasn't a problem.

Reading the interviewer's body language is key to a good interview. Interviewers will often make notes as they go through their list of questions. Their note taking will give away a lot of clues about whether you're on the right track with your answers. If you see them writing notes or ticking boxes next to the criteria they are evaluating you on, you're probably on the right track. On one occasion, after I started to answer a question, I noticed not one of the interview panelists were taking any notes. I spoke for a few moments, then stopped and said it looked like I wasn't answering their question correctly. It turns out I was right. After a quick clarification I was able to head down the right path.

Along similar lines, you can usually stop answering once you've seen the interviewers stop writing notes. Most interviewers won't interrupt you, so you've got to read their body language to avoid rambling on forever. If it looks like they're already satisfied that you know what you're talking about, take a moment to let them know that you have more to say about the topic if they want to hear it. For example, you could say:

> "I'm happy to explain how we used that product in other projects if you want to hear more about my experience with it."

If they're already confident you've answered the question well, they will usually take the opportunity to move on to the next topic.

Reading the interviewer's intentions when they pursue a question in more detail is a little trickier. Interviewers will ask follow up questions about a topic for one of two reasons:

1. **You might have given a really bad answer and they're trying to work out whether you just misspoke.** If you feel like the interviewer is staying on one point for too long, that's a clue you've probably given them an answer that raised some red flags about your knowledge. You can try to salvage the situation by being open about it, and ask if they could reframe the question so you can try again. Or you can just keep trying and if you don't get that job then do some additional research afterwards to find out what the correct answer should be.

2. **To probe how deep your knowledge of the topic goes.** If you feel like they are really diving into the inner workings and obscure knowledge of a topic, that's probably what is happening. This is a good sign, but it can also be a trap. At some stage the interviewer will either give up on that line of questioning, satisfied that you know more than enough

about the topic. Or, they'll eventually get to a level of detail or a scenario you're unfamiliar with. In the latter situation you must be honest and tell them when you've exceeded your understanding. Finding the limit of your knowledge is the goal of their questions, so there's nothing wrong with letting them know when the limit has been reached.

Questions about your hobbies and interests

Interviewers also like to ask about your hobbies and interests outside of work. Generally, what they want to see here is that you have interests that let you take your mind off work, de-stress, get outdoors, be around people, and so on. The only wrong answer here is a boring answer. Whatever your hobbies are, you need to put a positive spin on them. Don't just say "I play video games," tell them:

> "Well I'm saving for an overseas trip. Not sure where exactly yet, maybe Europe. So I stick to pretty cheap hobbies at the moment. Most nights I'll just play some video games or read a book. On weekends I try to get out for a walk or visit friends."

Most interviewers can identify with that. If your hobby is less common, like painting model trains in your basement, don't just say "I paint my model trains." Take the opportunity to show a side of yourself that may not have come across in the interview:

> "I like quiet hobbies that take my mind off work. For the last few years I've been collecting and painting model trains after someone gave me one for a birthday gift. It's quite relaxing, and one day the collection might be worth something and I can pass it along to my kids or sell some of it to pay for their college. I get together with other collectors every month, and we often take our sets to local fairs and raise money for charity by accepting donations to let people drive the trains around our tracks."

Whatever your story is, it needs to be the truth. If you don't have a good story because you don't have any hobbies or interests, I really encourage you to do something to change that. Remember, if they're hiring you, they'll be spending 40 hours a week with you. They probably have people in the team already who are into hiking, fixing up vintage cars, playing video games, or photography. If your hobby intersects with those who are already on the team, that's something that can work in your favor. Otherwise, they want to at least see that you're a regular human being who can interact with other human beings. If the choice comes down between two candidates of equal technical skill, the one who seems to have the more interesting personality will get the job.

The end of the interview

As the interview draws to a close you will often be asked if you have any questions of your own. The absolute wrong answer here is "no." You should always have questions. If you had questions that have already been answered throughout the interview, say so.

> "I was going to ask about your on-call arrangements for the team, but we've already discussed that."

Take the opportunity to probe for opportunities to improve your chances of landing the job. Some of my favorite questions to ask at the end of interviews are:

- What has been the biggest success for your team in the last six months?

- What will you be expecting from me in the first 30 days in this role?

- What's the first piece of advice you give to people when they join this company?

- What do you personally enjoy about working here?

Remember, you are interviewing them too. As the interview wraps up, I like to make a final statement along these lines:

"Thank you for your time today, I appreciate you inviting me here to discuss the role. I feel like I have a good understanding of what you're looking for, and that I can fit into your team well and add value with my skills and experience. What's the next step from here? Do you know when you'll be making a decision?"

Always make sure you know what the next step is. If you leave the interview without knowing what they will be doing next, and when you can expect to hear back from them, it makes it difficult to know when to follow up with them.

Interview feedback and responses

As an employer, I firmly believe that every job applicant deserves a response. There are job management tools available to recruiters and advertisers that make it simple to communicate with applicants. For unsuccessful applicants, my view is that applicants who were interviewed should be notified by phone. At the end of an exhausting round of interviews it's hard to get on the phone to deliver bad news, but it can help keep the door open with that candidate for future opportunities.

All other applicants can be notified by email. If the applicant was good enough to be short-listed I like to let them know that, and advise that we will keep their resume on file for future opportunities. If we suddenly have the need to hire again a few weeks or months after the last round of interviews, it's cheaper and easier to go to an existing pool of resumes than to go out to the public again.

Not all companies share my view though. Some companies will 'ghost' job applicants by never taking their calls, returning their emails, or providing any further communication after the interview. It's frustrating and unfair, but it happens. This is one reason why it's so important to leave the interview with a clear expectation of what the timeframe is for the next step in the hiring process. If they told you a decision would be made in two weeks, and it's now been four weeks with no response to your follow-up calls and emails, just move on with your life. They are probably just busy and don't want to take the time to notify unsuccessful candidates. There's a slim chance they're still deciding who to hire. Or perhaps they're in negotiations with their preferred candidate and haven't yet hired someone. But for your own mental well-being it's best to just accept the situation and keep looking for your next opportunity.

If you do hear back from a company letting you know that you were unsuccessful, you should ask for feedback. Many companies are reluctant to give specific feedback for fear of repercussions. One trick I used was to self-identify my weaknesses based on the job requirements. If the job asked for three years of VMware experience and I only had one year of experience at the time, I would ask if more VMware experience would have made me a stronger candidate. If there's no specific weakness you are aware of, you can ask them a safe question like "What could I work on to make me a stronger candidate if I were able to interview with you again in the future?"

9 Quick Tips for Interview Success

If you get to the interview stage for a job, it's a good sign, so you don't want to blow it by making simple mistakes. These nine tips will ensure you're setting yourself up for success:

1. Interview for any interesting sounding roles that come your way. Practice makes perfect.

2. Arrive 10-15 minutes early for the interview, but no more.

3. Make eye contact, give firm handshakes, and address the interviewers by their names.

4. Practice your 'tell us about yourself' answer so that it sounds natural and confident.

5. Be prepared to prove the technical skills and experience you claim on your resume.

6. Tell stories about your experience. Don't just recite the facts of the projects you worked on and the duties you performed.

7. Ask questions of the interviewers, especially near the end of the interview.

8. Always ask what the next step in the process will be, and when you can expect to hear back from them.

9. Keep applying for other jobs and attending other interviews. Nothing is guaranteed until you've got the job. And the more potential opportunities you can open up, the better your negotiating position.

SALARY NEGOTIATIONS

Some jobs are advertised with a fixed salary or hourly rate. Others have a range of numbers they are willing to offer for the role. When salary discussions come up during the interview itself, the golden rule is that the first person to say a number will lose the negotiation.

Negotiations are about leverage and compromise. Know what you want, what you're willing to compromise on, and what your limits are. The longer you've been in the industry the more leverage you will have. Unfortunately many IT professionals think they have no leverage. That may be true at the very beginning of your career when you're trying to get your first entry level job. But after that, you gain more and more leverage as your skills and experience grow.

Even in a slow job market you have some leverage if you're the best candidate that was interviewed. The gap between first and second place is usually quite large. Interviewers have already invested a lot of time going through a large pile of resumes and interviewing candidates. If you're good enough to get an offer, they're unlikely to let you walk away over a few thousand dollars in pay. And if they do, walk away happy knowing a company running on such razor thin profits that they can't afford to offer you a little more money is not a company worth working for.

Never tell the prospective employer or a recruiter what you're currently paid. The main reason for this is because it will limit the upper ranges of your offers. It doesn't matter what you're getting paid right now. It only matters whether you have the skills and experience to do the job they're hiring you for. If an employer learns that you currently earn $50,000, and they were prepared to pay up to $80,000 for the advertised role, they are very likely to try and get a bargain out of you by offering you $65,000 instead. After all, a 30% increase on your previously salary sounds very generous. But when you find yourself delivering $80,000 in value for $65,000 in compensation, you'll quickly become dissatisfied.

This is especially true if you're already aware of the salary range that the position pays. The recruiter may have provided this information to you during the recruiting process, or it may have come up in the interview. If your offer is not at the top end of that range then you should definitely negotiate for a higher offer. You're already the candidate they want to hire, and they've budgeted to pay that much. So why shouldn't you be paid that amount?

If you are asked about your current pay, redirect the question:

> "I'm paid appropriately for my position, but my skills have outgrown that role which is why I'm looking for

new opportunities. I'm interested to hear what you are offering for the advertised role."

If they ask you what you're expecting to earn in your next role:

> "I'm most interested in finding a job with a great team and technologies that I enjoy working with. I'm sure a company like yours will have an idea of the market rates for the role and will make an offer that is competitive."

If they push some more, asking why you won't tell them a figure:

> "I'm sure you have an idea of what this role is worth. Hearing the compensation offer from you will help me to understand the value that this role provides to your business, and that's important for me to know."

Those are uncomfortable things to say. In a salary negotiation, the person who is most uncomfortable will try to escape by giving a number. Hold out and make them put forward an offer for you. If it gets to the point where they insist that you propose a figure, perhaps threatening to withdraw you from consideration entirely, ask for an amount 20% more than you are willing to accept. Frankly once an employer puts that kind of ultimatum on me it tells me that they don't value me at all. Wasting everybody's time by running me through a gauntlet of salary negotiations doesn't bode well for later conversations about things that also cost money, such as training or replacement equipment. If I'm going to work for someone who doesn't value me then it better be for a lot of money. I add the 20% premium for that reason.

When you receive an offer, don't accept it immediately. The negotiation has just begun. Even if you're super happy with the offer you should take an evening or a few days to consider it. Make some notes about the details of the offer and what you want to negotiate. I've seen too many people gleefully accept an offer that is more than they currently make, only to realize later that they are actually underpaid for the role, or that the benefits and working conditions aren't great.

You should also work out the absolute minimum you're willing to accept, if you haven't already. That isn't the starting point for your negotiation. But you must go into the discussion knowing where the line is, below which you will decline the offer. Everything comes into play here. If you're going to lower your salary expectations, try to make up for it with better working conditions or a written promise of training. If the role has uncompensated overtime expectations (which they never should, in my opinion), make sure you're taking that into account when deciding the absolute minimum salary you would accept.

If you're reading this and thinking you're not in any position to negotiate, it's quite possible you're wrong. Many of us feel that way when we're applying for jobs. It's normal to feel like the company is doing us a favor by offering to hire us, and we should gratefully accept whatever they offer us. But in most cases you have more negotiation power than you think. You were selected from a pool of applicants, performed well in your interview, and the company has decided that you're the best candidate for the job. You won't get anything more if you don't ask.

Earlier in this chapter I wrote that you should keep applying for jobs and attending interviews, even when you have received an offer. Nothing is guaranteed until the job is officially yours, so keep pursuing opportunities. This will also help you in your negotiations in two ways. First, you can attend other interviews and let them know that you've already received an offer from another company. This can create a sense of urgency and might lead to a second offer coming to you quickly. Secondly, you can go back to the first company and continue the discussion by saying something like:

> "I like your company and the role seems like a good fit for me. I've also interviewed at another company and the salary/training/benefits/technology used there looks very promising. I'm expecting an offer from them

this week and I wanted to know if I have your best offer for this role so that I can make an informed decision."

This makes it clear that you're actively looking to get the best opportunity, and that other companies consider you a strong candidate. The prospective employer will react in one of a few ways.

One reaction might be to threaten to withdraw the offer, or put a deadline on it. I don't like to play that game, especially when there are multiple good opportunities available to me. In that situation I will stand my ground on needing more time, or decline the role. Getting pressured into making a decision often results in making a poor decision. You'll end up accepting an offer you're not entirely happy with, which leads to resentment and dissatisfaction in the role. Worse, if you then receive a better offer from elsewhere you've now put yourself in a situation where you need to withdraw acceptance of an offer, possibly before you've even started that job. It's a messy situation that can burn bridges with some companies.

Another reaction prospective employers can have is to ask you what you would change about the offer so that you'll accept it. This is another situation where you should avoid giving specific numbers. If you want the salary portion of the offer increased, ask them if they can do some more with the salary. If they won't budge on salary, ask if they can improve the training benefits, or write in some remote work days to the offer. This is all based on your earlier notes on what you actually want to receive, and what you're willing to accept as a minimum.

You can go back and forth on these details without ever stating a specific number. But if you feel that negotiations are stalled and the opportunity is at risk, now is the time to state what you want. This should be the top end of your desired compensation, because at best case they will accept it on the spot and you'll have gotten what you want. Maybe they would have offered more if you'd asked, but in my view if you get what you want then that is a reason to be happy. At worse they will counter with a lower offer. They may even tell you that it's the absolute best offer they can provide. In that case, as long as it's *above* my minimum *acceptable compensation*, I'm usually happy with the outcome.

Accepting an offer *lower than* your minimum *acceptable compensation* puts you in a bad position. Some employers will try to entice you with the prospect of pay raises once you're in the company and proving your worth. Unless the pay raises are written into your employment contract, and are based on achievable performance metrics, they're unlikely to materialize. I do not recommend accepting lower pay until you 'prove yourself' or for a probationary period. If you're doing the job from day one you deserve the full compensation. If it takes you months to ramp up to full productivity, then that is the fault of the company and the team that hired you for not having good onboarding processes for new employees. That cost should be on them, not you.

Before you accept an offer, all of the details of that offer should be provided to you in writing. Here in Australia it's often the case that a formal letter of offer is presented with the main points such as salary, work hours, and benefits. Acceptance of the offer is then conditional on reviewing the full contract that goes into full detail about the employment conditions. The letter of offer is a contract in the sense that you are agreeing to specific terms, but we can still withdraw acceptance if there's something in the full contract we don't like.

Do not quit your job until you have the new offer locked up. Here in Australia that generally means you've accepted an offer letter, and signed a full employment contract (yes, even for permanent full-time positions). In some other countries where employment contracts aren't used it's enough to just accept the offer letter. Until you have that clear agreement with the employer you should not resign from your current job. Too often I see people quit as soon as they have a verbal offer, then find themselves in a bad situation when the new employer moves the start date to the future. Or worse, withdraws the offer entirely.

Almost every contract I've signed has contained a non-compete clause that is unreasonable and unenforceable in this jurisdiction. After a few jobs I started objecting to the clauses by either crossing them out and initialing them, or by asking that they be modified before signing. I don't see the point in signing a contract that both parties know is unenforceable. Even if I could win a legal dispute over it, I could still go broke trying. So I prefer to have it fixed before it becomes a signed contract.

As a final note, let's just add a dose of reality and cover the unfortunate scenario in which you're desperate for a job. Maybe you're living in an economically depressed area. Maybe you've been out of the workforce for a few years and are lacking in recent experience. Maybe you have only one job offer in front of you, and it's a 'take it or leave it' offer with no room for negotiation. Perhaps you're relocating across the country and you don't have enough good contacts in the new city to open up better job opportunities for you. In any case, if you feel you have no choice but to accept what is being offered to you then you should go ahead and accept it. Survival trumps all other concerns at this point. It's not the end of your career, you'll have other opportunities in the future. Do what you have to do, and then regroup and try to improve your situation from there.

Getting Paid What You're Worth

This is the only time you get to seriously negotiate your compensation. Once you've accepted the job there is less incentive for the employer to offer you more. So don't miss this opportunity:

» Don't be the first one to say a number.

» Get everything in writing. Verbal promises such as a salary review after six months or the possibility of training courses mean nothing. Ask them for written confirmation of all the details so you can consider the offer in full.

» Look at the total compensation package. Salary (or hourly rate), flexible hours, remote work, mobile phone reimbursement, training budget, these are all things that are negotiable to make your compensation offer better.

» Don't accept an offer you're not happy with, hoping to get a pay raise or other benefits later on. Resolve to get what you want now, not later.

» If you accept a job that doesn't pay as much as you'd hoped, don't hold on to any resentment. Take the job for what it is, and keep looking for that better opportunity elsewhere.

STARTING A NEW JOB

If you've accepted a new job offer, congratulations! The hardest part is over. Before you begin the new job consider taking a short break for a few days or a week. If you can afford to do this it really helps to decompress and rest before you start with your new employer. This is especially important if you were burned out at your last job. Rolling straight into a new job without the opportunity to repair some of the physical and mental damage of your last job can get you off to a rough start.

But even if you were not burned out, starting a new job takes up a lot of energy as you will be exposed to a lot of new information all at once and will have to meet a lot of new people. Going into those first few days well rested is helpful.

Before you start in your new job find out exactly when and where you should report to on the first day. Ask for tips on public transport or parking. Some companies prefer you to come in a little later on the first day so they can get their morning routines out of the way before they deal with onboarding you.

You definitely don't want to be late on your first day. Do your research on how you're going to get there on time. If necessary, show up a little early and go grab a coffee nearby to kill some time. You can also ask what time you'll be expected to stay until. That's not to give the impression you're a clock watcher who heads out the door at exactly the time your work hours end. Instead, just let them know you need to plan your transport home, let your partner know what time to expect you, and so on.

Ask about dress codes if it hasn't already been explained to you. What you wore to the interview could be overdressed once you've actually got the job. If in doubt, wear what you wore to the interview and be ready to dress it down a bit by removing a tie or jacket.

Find out exactly who you'll be reporting to, and get their contact details to save in your phone. Get a backup contact as well, just in case your primary contact is unexpectedly absent. I've known many people who find themselves stuck in limbo when nobody at reception knows who they are, and the person they've been asked to report to is not answering their phone. Sitting around a reception area wondering if you're actually employed is not a nice feeling.

Most new jobs involve some terribly boring induction and onboarding procedures that you'll need to go through. This can range from a simple form to fill out and sign, all the way up to several days of mandatory training. I've fallen asleep in some of mine, and found it helps to get some extra sleep the night before, as well as keeping energy snacks such as trail mix on hand to get through the most boring parts of the day. It sucks, but that's life. Just go in prepared to do whatever is necessary to tick the boxes that people need ticked before they'll let you start doing your job.

Your access to the company's systems could also take some time to set up. It's quite common for new employee onboarding to be delayed by simple things like accounts not being ready, or a new computer that hasn't arrived.

Some IT organizations are excellent at bringing new hires up to speed quickly. They have good quality processes for all their tasks, pages of documentation neatly laid out in a Wiki, and great communication among themselves and with other teams. Sadly, those IT organizations are in the minority. The reality is often that you'll be given access to a ticketing system and a repository of half-written, out of date documentation, and told to just get involved.

The first work you'll receive will usually be the simplest and most boring tasks. These are the jobs that everyone else is sick of doing, so they get delegated to the new person to take responsibility for. A few lingering technical debt problems will likely also be lumped on you, things like finding a way to decommission some old legacy system that nobody else wants to touch. These tasks are good opportunities for you to become familiar with some of the grunt work that keeps the place moving, so approach it with an optimistic view. Set your ego aside, and don't look at it as work that's beneath you. It won't last forever. If you can complete the tasks, or automate them to be less time-consuming, you will get to move on to newer, more interesting work. And one day there'll be another new hire that has to go through the same process. You'll get to enjoy the freedom of delegating your least favorite work to them.

Take a paper notebook and keep notes for the first few weeks. A lot of new information will be coming at you and it will be impossible to remember it all: the names of servers, applications, teams, and key contacts, not to mention verbal instructions and other conversation snippets that are hard to recall in the overload of information that occurs early in a new job. Notebooks might seem old fashioned today, but they're still the best at what they do. Plus, it's more socially acceptable to make notes on paper during a conversation than to be tapping notes into an app on your phone.

You're also going to meet a lot of new people. For me this is the most exhausting part of starting a new job, trying to remember who people are and what they do. It doesn't help that I'm terrible at remembering names. I decided long ago to not be embarrassed by this and I just openly tell people I've forgotten their name when I interact with them the first few times.

Similarly if I'm brought into a conversation with people I haven't met yet, I will pause briefly to introduce myself and ask their name before we continue. It feels awkward at first, but trust me, it's far less awkward to just do it up front than to have to ask weeks later when you've already had a bunch of interactions with the person.

Try not to sit idle for long periods of time. When everyone around you is busy it's easy for you to get forgotten. Everyone gets wrapped up in their own work and doesn't think about the new person who has nothing to do. If you find yourself idle, go ask your team leader if there's anything they have for you. Or ask if there's someone you can shadow for a while to get some exposure to what others are working on. You can also ask to attend meetings to listen in and get up to speed on some of the projects that are going on.

Above all else, be prepared to feel dumb for a while. After you get comfortable with your new physical surroundings and the initial boring work you're given, you will start to realize there is a lot about the new company that you just don't know. Even if you understand the technical platforms that are being used, there'll be a lot of history and context that you aren't aware of. It's normal in the early stages of a new job to feel a slump in confidence and energy. Be patient. It can take one to three months to really feel useful and productive in a new job. Once you hit the three month mark there'll be enough keeping you busy that you'll start to feel confident again. After about six months you'll see opportunities to take ownership of some issues and your productivity should be hitting a high level.

New jobs are great networking opportunities. You should accept as many invitations as possible for coffee, lunch, after work social activities, and so on. If those situations make you uncomfortable, do a little research on small talk strategies. Remember, most people enjoy talking about themselves. So asking simple questions such as, "What is your team working on at the moment?" can get things moving easily.

DEALING WITH THE 'NEW JOB SLUMP'

Amateur marathon runners often suffer from post-race blues—an emotional crash in the weeks following a race. Even elite athletes can suffer from this. Professional sports men and women who retire suddenly find themselves lost without another race or season to prepare for. It's so common that in 2016, *The Atlantic* published an article about 'post-Olympic depression.' Not even winning a gold medal is a guarantee of avoiding the effects of total physical and emotional depletion, as life returns to an 'ordinary' state. In an interview with *ESPN*, retiring American basketball star Dwyane Wade, who has won multiple championships and achieved many other accolades during his career, said he plans to get therapy to help him make the adjustment to normal life.

Goals are funny things. We can, and should, set goals for ourselves. But it often happens that after we've achieved a short term goal it feels like we suddenly have nothing to look forward to. Which often leads us to quickly set a new one.

Don't forget, in achieving your goal, you likely had to sacrifice something to achieve it. Perhaps you spent less time with friends and family, or less time exercising. Your eating habits may have slipped as you valued speed and convenience over health.

Whatever you sacrificed, now is the time to make up for it. Have your fun for a while. And then set some new goals. It's important to note that those goals don't need to be work-related. Some of my goals over the last decade have included:

- Writing a book
- Running an ultramarathon
- Learning to play guitar again
- Building timber furniture from scratch
- Landscaping our gardens
- Watching every Star Wars movie in chronological order

It's also important to remember that some goals take more time than others to achieve. Building a wooden table took me a few days, whereas training to run an ultramarathon took six months.

The sense of satisfaction I got from each one was different as well. The table was for my kids' play room, and I still feel a sense of pride when I walk past it and see their Lego spread all over it. The ultramarathon training made me focus on good eating habits, changing my bad sleeping habits, and improving my time management so that I wasn't sacrificing other important things to get my training done. Plus the exercise was good for my body and soul.

If you find yourself in a slump after landing a job, take some time to reflect on what your next goal should be. It can be anything you want it to be. When you realize you have that freedom, that's when you know that you've achieved a life of happiness.

STAY OR GO

Your career in IT is going to face a lot of different challenges. When you find yourself in difficult and challenging situations you need to make hard decisions. The advice in this book will often boil down to two options:

1. Stay where you are and try to improve your situation

2. Go somewhere else and try to improve your situation

Not every bad situation needs you to leave your job to make things better. In fact, many problems can be solved by staying where you are and making a few changes. Let's face it, none of us are perfect. Changes we can make include:

- Updating our skills to make us better suited to our career

- Adjusting our expectations

- Adjusting our long term vision

You'd be surprised at the positive effect even a small shift in your thinking can have on how much you enjoy your job.

Changes can also be made with regard to how other people behave or perform. But it's much easier to change your own behavior and performance than it is to change that of other people. And pouring all your energy into trying to change others is often a fruitless exercise. Some problems just can't be solved no matter how hard you try. In situations like that, it's usually better to cut your losses, leave the company and go find a better job somewhere else.

As long as you're doing this:

- with your eyes open
- with awareness of what you're moving away from and what you want to move towards,

it's usually a good decision.

Knowing when to stay and when to go is the most important long term survival technique to master for a happy and successful IT career.

HOW TO QUIT A JOB

Over the first 16 years of my career I worked for nine different companies. In all but two situations (one company was acquired, and the new company went bankrupt; another company had me on a rolling contract, which eventually ended when they outsourced the role) I resigned from my job.

You could say I was pretty good at resigning from jobs. At the very least, it became an easy process for me. So much so, I sometimes forget that others don't really know how to resign from a job. Especially those who are resigning from the first job they got out of school.

Resigning is difficult from an emotional and psychological point of view. It's easy to second guess yourself:

- Are you leaving for the right reasons?
- Is there something else you should do to try and make the job work out?
- If you've accepted a new job, what if that job turns out to be worse than the one you're leaving?
- Are you letting people down by leaving?
- Should you consider counter-offers to stay?

From a process perspective, it can also seem quite confusing.

- Who do you resign to?
- Do you do it in person, or in writing?
- Is it too soon to leave this job?
- Should you find another job first?
- How much notice should you give?

Let's cover the emotional and psychological parts first. These present the biggest hurdle to successfully quitting a job, because they're the most likely to undermine you and cause you to change your mind.

First, you should never quit out of anger or frustration. If you're upset, go home and think about the situation. Talk it over with your partner, a mentor, or a trusted friend. Ideally this person will ask you the right questions to challenge your desire to quit. They aren't there to nod their head and agree with you no matter what, and they aren't there to talk you out of it. What you want is another perspective, and an objective view of the situation. Sleep on it. If you still feel strongly about quitting in the morning, it's likely you've made the right decision.

If you're worried you're going to let someone down—your manager, your teammates, your customers—I'm here to tell you that you won't. Sure, some of them will be disappointed. Losing a good team member always hurts. Hiring new people is expensive and frustrating at times. But those who care about you will be genuinely happy for you, knowing that you're making the right move for yourself.

And remember, this is a business. You're in the business of you. Your job is to make the best decision for yourself. If you leaving means your former teammates need to work a bit harder while they hire your replacement, it's not going to kill them. If they want to hold a grudge because you left and they got stuck doing your old work, perhaps their real problem is they don't want to work there either and they resent you for having the guts to leave.

All of us are replaceable. Don't take that the wrong way. It's not intended to be an insult. Everyone is replaceable. Life will go on without you.

You can quit a job at any time. There's no minimum period of employment where it becomes acceptable to quit. If a job isn't working out in the first few weeks, you can quit as long as you have a valid reason. Being given a boring task in your first week is normal. Being yelled at for making a mistake the first time you try to follow a new process is not normal. I've seen friends hired into teams that turned out to be toxic messes of narcissism and ego, who then stuck it out for months hoping things would improve. Things never did.

If you quit a job you've only been in for a short while, it's likely when you're interviewed for the next job that they'll ask why you're looking for a new job so quickly. The answer is simple:

> "The position was significantly different to that described in the interview. They aren't going to change it back to what it was described as, so I've decided to look for new opportunities."

Many situations are covered by that simple statement. You can then turn the conversation to the new role you're interviewing for:

> "I'm more interested in working with [insert attractive technology here], and this job offers that opportunity, so I submitted my application."

My shortest stint with a single company was three months. I took the job in good faith, intending to stay there for quite some time as they had a genuinely good corporate culture and work-life balance. In the first two weeks they announced a break up of the company into two smaller companies. Faced with the proposition of my job shrinking from managing 500 PCs to less than 100, I decided to look elsewhere. I spread the word amongst my friends, was referred for an interview for an internal vacancy, and accepted the new job. By the time my four weeks' notice was finished, it was exactly three months. I was later asked about that short stint during interviews, and was able to explain very simply that the company was shrinking to a size that would not challenge me and help me grow my career in the direction I wanted. It was never a problem in future interviews.

In Chapter 3 we're going to talk about personal finances. One of the tips is to save up an emergency fund to get you through a period of unemployment. The primary use case for your emergency fund is *unplanned* unemployment, such as being fired, or your employer going bankrupt. We'll discuss that shortly.

A secondary use case is so you can quit a job without first finding your next job. I have to note, this is not something I recommend. There's a risk you'll have trouble finding another job. This will create a gap in your employment history you'll need to explain in future job interviews. It will also put you under pressure to accept the first job you're offered. One which might not be any better than the job you just quit. So unless you urgently need to quit a highly toxic workplace, I recommend you find your next job first before quitting.

The process of quitting is simple. If your company has an HR department you can just ask them if there's a formal procedure you need to follow. Usually there isn't, and a simple email to your immediate superior is enough to start the process.

> "To whom it may concern, I hereby resign from my position as JOB TITLE for COMPANY. Per the terms of my employment agreement, I'm providing four weeks' notice, with my final day of employment to be [insert date here]."

I don't typically add reasons or feelings to my resignation letters. The letter is only intended to trigger the exit process, not explain the reasons behind the decision. I do recommend you keep it short and simple. If you want to make a positive statement about your time with the company, you could write:

> "I have enjoyed my time at COMPANY and greatly appreciate the opportunities that have been provided to me."

That's it. No need to elaborate on the details, air your grievances, or mention where you're going next. That's frankly none of their business. You don't need to write a long email about salary, working conditions, teammates, your boss, or any other factor that came into your final decision.

The four weeks of notice in my example above is typical for Australia. A notice period is written into most employment contracts. The actual notice period could be shorter or longer. Some people quit a job and give notice, but due to company policies (or emotional reasons by your former boss) are removed from the premises that day. The notice period becomes a paid vacation instead.

In senior roles it's sometimes necessary to provide a longer notice period. This should already be in your employment agreement. But if it isn't, and you feel like you're a critical person in an important role or project, you should consider discussing it with your boss first. That's assuming you are leaving on good terms, and you have a new job that is willing to wait for you.

Your employer might make a counter-offer to try and get you to stay. They might offer you more money, a new job title, or offer to fix whatever problems have led you to resign in the first place. I have two problems with counter-offers.

1. **More money doesn't solve whatever problems led to your decision to resign.**
   In fact, the company probably won't do anything else to solve those problems, and will just hope you stick with them for a while longer if they pay you more money.

2. **Since you've already accepted a new job somewhere else before you resigned, you would need to renege on the contract you signed with the new employer.** This is a bad move that could harm your chances of working with that company in the future. Furthermore, if a friend referred you for the new job opportunity, your decision to pull out after signing a contract will make them look bad as well.

Don't treat a resignation as leverage in a negotiation. You should not threaten to resign if you don't get what you want. If you've come to the point where you're willing to resign, negotiations are already over. It's time to walk away entirely.

In many companies it is standard procedure for the HR department to perform an exit interview with departing staff members. Exit interviews usually consist of a series of softball questions designed to extract certain answers from you and check for potential legal issues. The HR department is not the least bit interested in your gripes with your former manager or teammates. This is not an opportunity to fire a few shots to try and damage someone else's career as you head out the door. Seriously, they don't care. And anything you say can be dismissed as the rantings of a 'troublemaker' who 'wasn't a good fit' anyway.

When they ask you, "Why are you leaving?", they don't want to hear "My manager is incompetent, and has no idea how to run a technical team." Save it for the bar later with your mates.

So what should you say instead? Here are a few examples.

Q: Why are you leaving your current position?

As tempting as it is to blast your former manager, or your annoying teammates, focus on the benefits of your new position:

> "I was offered the opportunity to work with some new technologies that aren't on the roadmap here at COMPANY. It's a direction I want to move in with my career, so I decided to take up the offer."

You should go in to the exit interview prepared to give a few examples of things you did like about working for the company. I assume at some stage you were happy there, even if that only lasted a few weeks.

Q: What did you like most about your job?

You can give a simple answer about something that you achieved, no matter how big or small it was. Remember, you're leaving the company, not applying for a job there. You're under no pressure to impress them with your accomplishments as you walk out the door.

> *"I'm proud of the work I did on the BIG PROJECT to upgrade the IMPORTANT SYSTEM."*

Any questions about things you didn't like should be approached with caution.

Q: What did you dislike most about your job?

Your instincts here will tell you to complain about the pay, or the hours, or the ten-year-old IT equipment that is barely staying alive. Even if the HR person believes what you say, they're not likely to be in a position to do anything about it. Again, use something good about your new role to highlight any issues you had.

> *"The long hours were putting a strain on my family life. My new role has a fixed on-call roster so I will only be doing after hours work one week per month."*

Sometimes they will ask an open question to draw out any other issues.

Q: Is there anything else we could have done to keep you from leaving?

If you want to tell them a pay raise or better working conditions would have made you happy, by all means do so. But deliver the message in a way that shows you made good faith attempts to attain those things.

> *"I spoke to my manager about increasing my salary to a more competitive rate for this market, which would*

have helped me with the increase in our cost of living over the last few years. He said there was no budget for pay raises, so that's when I began looking for other opportunities."

When I resigned from one of my former employers, I ended up in an exit interview with a particularly aggressive HR officer. They seemed intent on getting a specific answer out of me, and kept pressing me on the question of why I was leaving. Eventually I had to say:

"There's really no single reason for me leaving. Sometimes we just need a change in life. This is one of those times."

When you quit a job, you're going to get asked questions by your colleagues.

- Why did you quit?
- Where are you going?
- Can I come with you?

It can be uncomfortable if you don't want to share too much information, particularly if you're joining a competitor. This is a private matter for you, and you should feel free to answer with as much or little information as you want. Even if you're discussing it with people you consider to be your friends, workplace gossip spreads fast.

I treat these questions a lot like the HR exit interview.

Q: Why are you leaving?

"I got an offer to work with TECHNOLOGY X, which I've been interested in for a while. It's a bit closer to home and they offered a bit more money so I decided to go for it."

Q: Where are you going?

"I'd rather not say right now, but if you check my LinkedIn profile in a couple of weeks you'll see it."

Don't get me wrong. If you want to proudly announce you've been hired by Google, or Microsoft, or Facebook, by all means do so. Just don't feel pressured to reveal more than you want.

As you approach your last day there are usually some other tasks to close off your employment. I recommend you pack up your personal belongings and take them home with you a few days before your last day. If you think your resignation is going to have you marched out the door immediately, start taking your personal belongings home a few days beforehand so all that's left are a few essentials to pack up. After you've resigned, have another team member observe you while you pack up so there can be no accusations of theft.

Don't delete work emails or files. Those are company property and should be left for your former employer to do whatever they need to do for compliance purposes. If you have any work in progress, drafts, notes, or anything else that will be useful to your teammates, hand those over. You should also write out a list of any ongoing projects that someone else will need to take responsibility for, and hand those over as well.

On your last day, hand in any remaining company property, and then you're all finished.

Once you've left the company, you owe them nothing. Harsh as that sounds, your full attention should now be given to your new job and to maintaining the quality of your life. In some circumstances, a former employer will contact you to ask you for information or assistance. Maybe they've forgotten why a system was implemented the way it was, or something has broken and they can't get it working.

Some IT pros will tell you that this is an opportunity to make a little side income by billing your former employer for your time. In many cases, this is true. For me, it's not worth the time or the paperwork, not to mention the possible insurance problems it creates. I value my free time more than any amount of money a former employer would be willing to pay me.

If it's a good friend calling, then of course I'll help them. But I'm not personally in the habit of helping out every former employer, paid or free. You will need to make a judgment call for yourself.

HOW TO HANDLE LOSING A JOB

Losing your job sucks, big time. Even if it's a job you don't like, it sucks to have it taken away from you at a time that isn't of your choosing.

Sadly, it's a situation we all need to be ready for. Whether you get fired, lose a job to redundancy or bankruptcy, or are forced to resign for reasons outside your control, the result is the same. An unplanned loss of income which can put immense pressure on your personal life.

It must be noted that **losing a job due to layoffs** and **being fired** are two separate scenarios.

Losing a job due to layoffs

Layoffs tend to be an impersonal decision, perhaps an outcome of downsizing or outsourcing. Layoffs can happen in multiple rounds. So even if you survive a round of layoffs, keep your eyes and ears open for signs of another one coming. Managers don't like to give advance warning of layoffs. (They want to try and maintain morale and productivity, and prevent people from jumping ship too soon.)

Often your immediate manager will not even know about layoffs until the day they happen. Your manager will be told to cut the team by 20%, and have a matter of hours to decide who will stay and who will go. No matter how good a friend they are, there's no advance warning they can give you.

Poor financial performance is an obvious sign of impending layoffs. If your company is making sudden announcements about hiring freezes or halting all non-essential travel, it often means they're in panic mode and are trying to stop the bleeding while they work out what to do next. One company I worked for decided to stop buying biscuits for the tea room, and cut the milk order in half as well. For a few hundred dollars in savings it did immeasurable harm to morale in the team.

Bringing in outside consultants to look for 'cost savings' or 'efficiencies' is another red flag. If your company inserts a new manager into the upper levels of the organization who has no direct reports, go and take a look at their LinkedIn profile. A recent work history of short, three to six month engagements as a consultant to various companies is a sign that they specialize in the type of consulting that leads to layoffs.

A sudden interest in the finer details of your day-to-day activities is also a warning sign. External IT providers work on a billable basis and are used to tracking their time. Internal IT staff usually do not have to track their time other than total hours worked in the day. When layoffs are imminent, particularly when outsourcing is being planned, the company will ask IT staff to start tracking how much time is spent on each job ticket. The intention is to get some visibility into the activities that IT is performing such as reactive support, proactive maintenance, projects, and reporting, to begin discussing pricing with outsourcing providers. In my entire career I've never seen or heard of a case where internal IT staff were required to start tracking time without it eventually leading to layoffs and outsourcing.

As a general rule, whenever I hear of layoffs happening in my team or anywhere else in the company, I quietly update my resume and get in touch with a few recruiters and contacts in the industry. Remember, there's no harm in having a conversation with a recruiter and even attending a few interviews to see what better opportunities might be out there. And if your friends know your job is at risk they can also keep an eye out for opportunities for you. More than once I have had friends tell me to give them a call if I get caught up in layoffs. It's not a guarantee of a job, but it's nice to know that people are ready to help you when you need it.

Being fired

Being fired is quite different. They say most people who are fired will see it coming long before it happens. Some people probably miss the signs though. And some other people probably stress about what they think is their impending termination, even when it's not actually about to happen.

There are a few situations that can get you fired. It should go without saying that if you commit a criminal act you're going to get fired. Similarly, if you breach a crucial industry regulation you can also expect to lose your job over it. Breaching internal company policy can also get you fired. The best way to avoid these situations is to be aware of the regulations and policies under which you operate.

Reading company policy manuals is boring, but necessary. It's tempting to gloss over them and treat them as a box-ticking exercise when you start working for a company. I do recommend you take the time to read them properly. You can't plead ignorance if you get caught doing something you were told was against policy.

Mistakes can and do happen without job loss, but gross negligence will usually lead to termination of employment. Especially if your negligence has a direct cost or exposes the company to liability.

While there are some companies who will treat your $100,000 mistake as a $100,000 investment in your training, (there's a good chance you won't make that mistake again!), most will sack you on the spot.

The best way to avoid being negligent is to have a healthy respect for the value of risk assessment and procedures. Too often I see IT professionals making changes under pressure without properly understanding the risks. If you can't perform the risk assessment yourself, enlist the aid of your teammates or your manager. There's no need for anyone to make a high risk decision on their own.

Similarly, there is no need for you to take personal responsibility for someone else's insistence on a high-risk change being made. Having a documented group consensus, or an order from a superior to do something despite the risks you've communicated, is one of the best insurance policies you can have. People talk about 'covering your ass' for a reason. It matters.

Ongoing poor performance is one of the main causes of job loss. This is a tricky area because of what's commonly known as 'imposter syndrome.' A lot of people constantly feel like they're in over their head, underqualified for their job, and always at risk of being exposed as an 'imposter' and fired. This is mostly a mental problem. When you're surrounded by people who are already intimately familiar with an environment and seem confident and comfortable in everything they are doing, any gaps in your own skills and knowledge seem huge to yourself.

It's important you don't allow imposter syndrome to have a real impact on your performance. Understand that appearances are often deceiving. Everyone struggles with self-doubt. But you can overcome it with simple productivity habits, time management, and communicating well with others. Those topics are discussed in later chapters of this book.

Genuinely poor performance will be brought to your attention. The regular feedback you get from your peers and leaders will include criticism. But not all critiques mean you are performing poorly. A good team will use peer review and critiques as a way to boost performance from good to great. Just because your peers were able to identify an improvement doesn't mean your work was bad, just that it could be better. We should always strive to improve, and criticism is part of that process.

Feedback about actual poor performance should be specific and actionable. If your manager is telling you they expect you to be able to process a certain number of tickets, or meet a certain service level agreement (SLA), that is a target you can work towards. If the feedback is vague, and you're just being asked to 'do better' and meet a non-specific benchmark of acceptable performance, that's a tough situation to be in. If you can help it, don't walk away from any such meetings without a clear understanding of what is expected of you.

Many companies have systems known as PIP, or performance improvement plan. These are formalized performance management processes that usually involve the HR department and your immediate manager. Your company will tell you a PIP is intended to address performance issues and turn an employee back into a productive member of the team. This is partially true in the sense that replacing employees is an expensive process. Keeping the staff you already have is preferable to firing them and hiring someone new who needs to go through all the onboarding and familiarization phases of employment before they become productive.

But a PIP is also an expensive process and uses up a lot of time. Companies don't enter into them lightly, and often do it as a last resort to begin the process of firing someone without the risk of unfair dismissal claims. If you find yourself in the PIP process with performance targets that seem unreasonable or impossible to achieve, that's a sign that the company is planning to terminate you. If you can leave on your own terms beforehand it may be a better outcome for you.

There are three things you must do to prepare for the possibility of losing your job:

- Save up an emergency fund
- Maintain your employability
- Know your legal rights and entitlements

The first two points are discussed further in the next chapter of this book. The third point I will cover here with the following caveat: I'm not a lawyer of any kind, let alone an employment lawyer. I only know what I've learned from reading, understanding, and negotiating my own employment contracts.

Legally our situations will all be different, because of different employment laws around the world. If you have any questions about your specific situation you should speak to a lawyer in your area. A short consultation is usually a few hundred dollars, unless you can find someone offering free consultations or a community legal service. Spending that much money will be difficult for some people, and I know more than a few who have simply walked away from a situation even though they were probably entitled to some compensation such as a severance payment. They just couldn't afford the money and the stress of a legal dispute.

Here in Queensland, where I live, we have different workplace laws to other parts of Australia. And Australia on the whole has different workplace laws than the USA and other countries.

Every employment contract that I've signed has contained these main points:

- Salary and entitlements (e.g. paid vacation days, sick days, mobile phone and other allowances)
- Probationary period (usually three months)
- Termination conditions (e.g. one week's notice required by either party during probation, or four weeks' notice required by either party after probation)

With those details in my contract I always knew where I stood, and my employer knew where they stood. The company couldn't sack me on the spot without paying me out the four-week notice period plus my unused vacation time. Losing your job is less scary when you know you're owed four to eight weeks of salary to help you survive while you find your next job. Similarly, I couldn't walk out the door without giving four weeks' notice, or risk forfeiting my unused vacation time and any remaining salary.

Those employment conditions were also backed by employment laws protecting me from things like forced redundancy and unfair dismissal. If a company chose to make my role redundant, I would be entitled to my normal severance payments plus an additional payment based on the number of years I have worked for that company. Similarly, the company could not fire me for no good reason. If they did, I would have grounds to pursue an unfair dismissal claim which could result in compensation or the reinstatement of my job.

None of these are ideal situations, but knowing what your rights are, and what you've agreed to during your employment contract negotiations, helps you prepare for unplanned loss of employment.

Of course, contracts and employment laws can't save you in every case. Back in the mid-2000's when the global financial crisis hit, the company I was working for was in a precarious financial situation. The economic downturn was enough to tip us into bankruptcy. There's a lot to the story, but how it affected me and my teammates was that one day we just didn't get paid our salaries. It actually took us a few days to notice, because most of us just assumed we got paid and rarely checked to make sure the money had arrived. It was my wife who first noticed that my pay was missing, and everyone else in the team quickly confirmed theirs was missing as well.

For me, not getting paid was a concern, but not a crisis. My wife and I had a young child and a mortgage to think about. But my wife still had the income from her business, and we had enough money saved to survive for a while.

For some of my colleagues who lived week to week, however, the situation was more severe. They needed the money badly and were faced with a difficult choice. If they quit, they would lose access to unemployment benefits and other government funds that had been created to protect employees from corporate bankruptcies. If they simply walked away, they could also be accused of job abandonment, losing access to their entitlements if the company somehow managed to recover from its financial problems. If they stayed, they didn't know when their next pay check would arrive.

Ultimately the decision was made for us. After three agonizing weeks, the company formally announced insolvency, and our employment was terminated.

Now things got even trickier. Another company bought the failed business, and offered some of my colleagues a job. Those colleagues were put in another tough position. If they turned down the job, they would not be entitled to unemployment benefits or other compensation payments, other than the salary and entitlements they were owed by the bankrupt company. And as one of many creditors of a failed business, there was not much hope of seeing a single dollar. When your only other choice is to take a job with a company that you don't want to work for, there is really no right answer.

Some of my colleagues took the offered jobs just for the steady pay check. Some turned them down and tried their luck in a depressed job market, knowing they were forfeiting all government assistance. The rest of us started our job searches, and also made our applications to the government for compensation, a process which took nearly two years for me. That's a long time to wait for what you're entitled to.

TIP: Dealing With Job Loss

The safest approach to job security is to assume that you have none, and that you can lose your job at any time for any reason. This puts you in a mindset of preparation and readiness, instead of fear and panic.

> » Check your employment contract and legal entitlements so that if you lose your job you know what you are entitled to receive in terms of notice period and payouts.

> » Save up an emergency fund that will cover your living expenses for three to six months. If possible, get insurance coverage for income protection in the event of unexpected illness or injury that prevents you from working.

» Never lash out, bad mouth, or seek to damage the reputation of a former employer. The worst thing I have ever said about a former employer is that they were not a good fit for me and I probably wouldn't apply for roles there in future. If you want to privately make comments about a former employer or manager, just keep in mind that anything you say or write about them will be repeated to someone else eventually.

» Keep your resume and LinkedIn profiles updated, even when you're not looking for jobs. I give mine a review every three to six months to add notes for any interesting new skills or projects that I've acquired in that time.

» Write a list of the first five people you would call if you lost your job. In Chapter 3 we'll discuss why your personal network is important.

CHAPTER 2 RECAP

Before trying to break into the IT industry, it's helpful to research both the industry and the geographic area you intend to work in to see what skills are in high demand.

- Always have an up-to-date resume on hand, along with a willingness to tailor your resume for every specific job application.

- Understand how the recruitment industry works (what motivates recruiters) and maintain a good relationship with recruiters at all times. You never know when you're going to need them, and sometimes they will present you with opportunities you never imagined.

- The easiest way to become more proficient at job interviews is to do as many job interviews as you can.

- In interviews, ensure you are prepared with good answers to common interview questions.

- Remember the golden rule of salary negotiations: the first person to say a number loses.

- When starting a new job, prepare to be given grunt work and maybe even feel bored and flat.

- Never quit a job out of anger and frustration. Always give yourself the chance to sleep on it.

- When resigning from a job, keep communications simple and free of emotion.

- Be prepared to answer common exit interview questions with grace.

- Be aware of the impending signs of layoffs and prepare accordingly.

- Be aware of situations that could lead to you being fired and adjust your performance accordingly.

- Always have an emergency fund on hand to deal with unexpected unemployment.

CHAPTER 3
THE BUSINESS OF YOU

Your career is a business, and you're the CEO. That means when it comes to building a successful career, the buck stops with you.

Yes, you'll get some help along the way.

- You'll find friends and mentors who give you great advice.
- You'll find employers who are willing to invest in your growth.
- And you'll be the recipient of the occasional dose of luck and good fortune.

But ultimately it's up to you.

- You need to cultivate those friendships and relationships with mentors.
- You need to sell employers on why they should invest in you.

- And when luck comes your way, you need to make the choice to grab the opportunity and make the most of it.

Take charge of your career. If you don't, you'll be stuck fulfilling other people's needs, and never your own.

BUILDING YOUR NETWORK

With the exception of my very first job in the IT industry and then one contract role later on, every other job I received involved a recommendation, referral, or even a direct hire by someone who knew me. In other words, my personal network is what opened the doors that kept me employed for more than 18 years.

I'm not ashamed or embarrassed by that. In fact, I'll openly admit that applying for publicly advertised jobs and competing purely on the strengths of your resume and interviewing skills is a tough process I would happily avoid. My success rate was fairly typical of the people I know as well.

- Only the most exceptional candidates have a near 100% success rate for interviews leading to offers.
- Very good candidates are successful around half the time.

- It's most common to have a success rate under 20%, sitting five to ten interviews to get an offer. (People just don't talk about it that much because they see it as a failure.)

Aside from the two jobs I landed without a personal recommendation, there were only two occasions where I went through the entire selection process for a publicly advertised role and got all the way to an offer. In both cases I declined as I had another offer with a company where a friend or former colleague was recommending me.

In all other cases I was eliminated from consideration for publicly advertised roles before getting to the offer stage. The reasons were varied.

Sometimes no reason was given.

Other times I was told that the organization was too small and I would be bored in the role. (Having previously worked for a large multinational organization was more harmful than helpful in finding other jobs later, as it turned out.)

In several cases I later found out (through informal channels) that the person selected over me had an insider who was able to recommend them. This doesn't upset me since I have also won roles on the basis of an insider recommendation in many cases. It's a competitive advantage that can't be understated. And it can mean getting access to job opportunities that are never publicly advertised, which makes the entire process a lot easier.

This is why your personal network is one of the best assets you can build throughout your career. Don't underestimate its value. And don't underestimate who can be a good contact for you in the future. Even those people who you aren't directly working with every day will form opinions about your expertise and professionalism. Just because Sue the DBA never has to interact with you about the servers you manage, that doesn't mean Sue won't form an opinion based on what John (the other DBA) says about you from his own interactions. If John complains about your attitude, or about everything taking forever to get finished, Sue will form that impression herself as well.

One of the simplest ways to build your professional network is to talk to people. For some of you who are natural introverts that sounds like a nightmare scenario. I'm somewhat introverted myself. Going to a meetup or conference with strangers is an uncomfortable situation for me, but I'm okay once I get to know people a little. So over the years I've focussed on getting over that initial hurdle of being among strangers and developed some techniques for establishing that initial connection with people.

In a room of strangers I make it a point to introduce myself to two people. That's all it takes. Two is important, because if you only introduce yourself to one person and they leave early or just turn out to be a dead end at least you've got someone else to keep chatting to. Two is also not too many people for an introvert like me (who is also bad at remembering names). Pick someone who is standing alone and say hello.

> "Hi there, I'm Paul. I don't know anyone here so I figured I'd just introduce myself."

Try not to make it super awkward for them. If they've just taken a bite of food and have a drink in their other hand it's going to be pretty hard for them to shake your hand and speak to you. If you feel like you've created the world's most awkward meeting between strangers, hit the eject button with a quick excuse.

> "Oh I'm sorry, I don't mean to be rude but I just realized I forgot to let my partner know that I'll be home late. Excuse me, I'll just go make a quick call."

If there's nobody standing alone then you're going to need to interrupt a conversation. Otherwise you risk standing alone until someone else takes the initiative to talk to you. For me that's an even more uncomfortable situation than talking to strangers, so I do my best to avoid it. Interrupting people in a deep conversation can come across quite rude, so pick a group of two or three people who look like they're just making idle chit chat.

> "Hi there. Sorry to interrupt, but I don't know anyone here so I figured I'd just introduce myself. I'm Paul."

It's hard to be spontaneous when you're nervous. So don't go into social situations completely unprepared. Have some small talk and conversation starters ready to use. Everyone can introduce themselves and say where they work. Beyond that it takes some grease to get the conversation moving.

Remember that above all else, people love talking about themselves. Give people an opportunity to share their opinions, brag about something they're proud of, or gripe about something they're unhappy about, and the conversation starts to flow very easily. Personally, I don't like to be the one listening to gripes and complaints, so I prefer to ask for people's opinions or recent victories.

> "So what are you working on at the moment? Oh that sounds interesting. Is that going to fix the problems with ..."

Giving people the chance to share their knowledge with you is also a good way to get them talking. Ask them to help you understand a piece of technology you're struggling with. Or, if the conversation is more social and less work-related, ask them something else.

"I finished the last episode of Westworld last night. Did you see it? I'm still not sure I fully understand why ..."

If television isn't your thing, ask for a recommendation about something else.

"I'm planning a night out for my partner and I. Does anyone know a great Thai restaurant we could go to?"

Not only do people love sharing their knowledge, but they love to hear that their knowledge was useful.

"Hey thanks for that restaurant recommendation. The food was amazing. I owe you one."

They'll appreciate knowing that their recommendation was a good one. And they will also appreciate knowing you are someone they can come to when they next need help with something. Having others come to you for help gives you more opportunities to build strong connections with them. This isn't manipulative, it's just building connections through reciprocity.

It's important in any social situation to know why you're there. The examples above are small talk I would make with colleagues. But if I'm at a professional meetup, people usually don't want to talk about television shows and restaurants. They want to talk about the topic of the meetup. But you can still use the same techniques.

> "So how are you using Product X at the moment? Oh that sounds interesting. Are you using the new Feature Y yet?"

Again, give people the chance to share their knowledge with you.

> "I've been looking at new Feature Y today actually. I'm not sure I fully understand why it would be better than using ..."

And, just like the restaurant question, you can ask for recommendations.

> "We've been looking for something to help us monitor our system. Does anyone know a good product we can try out?"

Above all, be yourself. If you're not a natural joker, don't let nerves fool you into thinking you need to throw witty remarks into the conversation. If you don't know the answer to a question, don't stress out thinking you need to impress people with your knowledge. Admitting you don't know something and asking others for their thoughts is yet another way to keep the conversation flowing.

If you simply feel you can't go into a meetup or other social situation without some backup, take a friend or colleague with you. Having someone there who can take up some of the conversation load can help you to preserve some energy and not look frantically for an exit when things get overwhelming. Invite someone who is a little less introverted than you are. You could even invite someone who is a total extrovert. But if you're an introvert like me it can feel even more intimidating tagging along with a super extroverted person.

Ever felt trapped in a conversation you just want to get out of? I find it best to hit the eject button as hard as possible to avoid any awkwardness. A simple "Well it was nice to meet you, I'm going to go grab another drink/find a restroom/introduce myself to the meetup organizers" should do the trick. If it looks like they're going to tag along with you, pull out a secondary excuse. "Actually I need to make a quick phone call first. See you next time!"

To grow your network, start with the people around you. The best people to get to know are those you work with every day. That includes your immediate teammates, the other teams you interact with, and any key individuals in your customer base that you deal with regularly. Go for a walk to get coffee together. Sit in the break room at lunch instead of eating alone at your desk. Accept the invitation (if you can) for a drink after work on a Friday. In each situation, use your small talk starters to get the conversation flowing if you need to.

As your network starts to grow it's important to remember that making connections is just the first part of the process. The second part is keeping up with your existing connections. It's easy to stay in touch with the people you work with. After all, you see them almost every day. But the people who no longer work with you, or that you meet at outside events, takes a little more effort. If you see them regularly at the same meetups and events, you can make a point of having a quick chat. If you're not running into each other at events, take the time to invite them to lunch, coffee, or a drink after work.

And remember, networking is a two way street. If you're invited to catch up, try and say yes enough times to maintain those strong connections with people. You don't have to go drinking every Friday with people, but every now and then you can accept that lunch invitation, meet for a coffee, or stay back for one beer. You can say yes to joining their sports team, or meeting up online for some gaming. People will come and go from your professional network over time, so it's not like you need to maintain connections forever. But that one year you had fun playing basketball with someone could mean the difference five years from now when you're a candidate for the job you want.

Getting Started With Professional Networking

Your network will open doors to the best jobs available, and keep you employed when the job market is at its worst. The more you network, the easier it becomes. Here are some tips to grow and maintain your professional network:

» Get away from your desk for an in-person meetup (coffee, lunch, a drink) with at least one person you work with every week.

» Catch up in-person with at least one person you don't work with each month. If you can handle more, make it one per week.

» Choose a regular meetup or user group that you can regularly attend and stay connected to via mutually interesting topics.

» Get involved in hobbies and activities (e.g. sports, gaming, photography, charity work) with people in the industry.

MOVING UP THE CAREER LADDER

For most people, a successful career includes some form of ascension from a lower level job to a higher level job. Help desk people want to become systems administrators. Admins want to become architects. Juniors want to become seniors.

While I think there is nothing wrong with sustaining a long career at whatever level makes you happy, I respect that most people want to move up the ladder at some stage. Thinking back to my own career progression and the other people I've worked with over the years, there are some common elements that appear in all our stories.

Moving up in your career tends to happen in one of two ways:

1. You're offered a promotion or higher level job by your current employer based on how well you're performing.

2. You apply for a higher level job, either internally or at another company, and are the successful candidate who receives an offer.

If you expect your current employer to offer you a higher level role, the first point I want to make here is that you must be doing your current job well. Yes, everyone knows someone who got promoted despite their mediocrity. But, that's not the path you're looking to take.

My first job was working in a help desk team. In the first year I was offered an opportunity to take on a role with more responsibilities in a new project team. That opportunity, and every other internal promotion opportunity after it, came about because of a few things I did consistently well:

- Being reliable and showing attention to detail. If you have five things you're responsible for, do those five things exceptionally well before you ask to be trusted with more.

- Being a good communicator with other colleagues and customers. If you can demonstrate you can get along with a diverse range of people in different circumstances, then people will see you as an asset.

- Showing an interest in learning more about the technologies I was supporting. Don't settle for remembering answers to questions, and solutions to problems. Work on a deeper understanding of the products you're working with, and learn how to analyze and troubleshoot unfamiliar problems.

- Asking to be involved in projects that need someone to do low-level tasks. Yes, this means doing 'grunt work.' But it exposes you to more learning opportunities, and grows your reputation as someone who gets the job done.

As you move higher up the ladder into more senior roles, some additional characteristics become important:

- The ability to zero in on the correct solution quickly. Whether it's troubleshooting a problem, designing a system, or writing code, senior professionals are expected to quickly analyze and eliminate incorrect solutions and find the right one fast.

- The ability to anticipate and address unknown problems. Senior IT professionals are expected to do less reactive work and be more proactive in seeking out problems to solve and improvements to make. They are also expected to be pragmatic and avoid change for the sake of change.

- The ability to teach, mentor, and bring out the best in others. Senior IT professionals don't operate in an isolated bubble away from everyone else. They're expected to guide others to outcomes and support them when needed. They're expected to lead teams and apply the right people to problems, not just the right technology.

Those characteristics are what will open doors for you to higher level opportunities in your company. But not all companies have room for you to move up. It may be that they have exactly the right number of senior staff that they need, and you face a long wait for someone to be promoted or resign before you get the opportunity for advancement.

Fortunately those same characteristics are what will open doors for you to move on to new roles at other companies. In fact, it's more likely that you will need to look outside your current employer to find the promotion you desire. It can be hard to leave a company you like working for, and people you like working with. But if you've outgrown your role and you have your sights set on bigger things, then that is just what you will need to do.

One of the advantages of moving to a new company is that it puts you in a better position to negotiate your compensation. A promotion within the same company will rarely come with a 30-50% salary increase. There's no good reason for that. If you're worth more money in the market, then you should get what you deserve. But a lot of employers are reluctant to give such a big pay increase to an existing employee. When you apply for roles with other companies, however, you get the opportunity to negotiate without the prospective new employer knowing your current salary.

Whether you're looking for an internal promotion or you're looking elsewhere for higher level roles, remember it is extremely rare for opportunities to just be handed to you out of nowhere. If you're toiling away hoping that one day someone will notice and promote you, you could be waiting for a very long time. Make your intentions known. Ask your boss what it will take to be considered for a promotion. Formulate a plan to meet those requirements. If they don't come to the party with the promotion you want, take your skills to the market instead.

Don't be shy about job hopping. It can be a fast road to success. There are no bonus points for taking longer to get where you want to be. If you're ready for that higher level role today, go out there and get it.

UPSKILLING AND STAYING EMPLOYABLE

Every job offers training and professional development. Almost none of them actually provide it. The lure of training has been dangled in front of me more times than I can remember. In nearly 20 years of working for other companies I attended a grand total of four technical training courses paid for by my employer. There would be a few seminars and free workshops as well. But any way you slice it, I was sent on paid training about once every four years.

When I eventually worked out my employers weren't going to invest heavily in my professional development I started doing it myself. On a recent decluttering of our house I found dozens of old technical books and video training courses on DVD that I'd purchased. I'd spent thousands of dollars on them. Some of them were good, some of them not as useful.

Today an IT professional can get by with ebooks and online training courses. We can carry our entire training library everywhere we go on a laptop or mobile device. I still spend anywhere from $500-$2000 a year on professional development today. I'm fully aware that's a lot of money and out of reach for many people in the industry. And that's fine. I'm not going to tell you that a $2000 annual investment is necessary. In fact, you can get away with spending almost nothing on training, even if your employer is not contributing anything, and still pick up new skills all year round.

First, let's break down how an IT professional can look at skills development. There are two types of skills IT pros should work on:

1. **Technical skills** such as networking, databases, security, and specific vendor products.

2. **Soft skills** such as business writing, time management, leadership, teamwork, and so on.

Technical skill development

Your technical skills fall into two categories: knowledge, and experience. In total there are four types of technical skills you possess:

1. **Conceptual awareness** is your knowledge of how things work. This includes your understanding of things such as application models, architecture and design patterns, security concepts, and best practices. You can develop and maintain your conceptual awareness through reading books and white papers, watching videos and presentations, and participating in communities of your peers such as forums, Facebook groups and Reddit. These communities often discuss concepts in a product-agnostic manner, such as discussing security concepts and best practices like least-privilege access.

2. **Capability awareness** is your knowledge of what a product or service can do. This extends your conceptual awareness by providing you with an understanding of how a specific product achieves an outcome. Keeping with the previous example of least-privilege access, your capability awareness would include an understanding that Microsoft Windows and Active Directory

are capable of supporting a least-privilege access model, whereas your legacy phone system that can only be logged into with full admin rights is not capable. You can develop and maintain your capability awareness by following news, blogs, and RSS feeds. For example, software vendors often release blog posts and PR statements to journalists that their product is capable of something, but don't go into technical detail on exactly how they do it. It doesn't consume a lot of time or mental storage to stay up to date on what products are capable of. Maintaining your awareness of capabilities means you can confidently select products for evaluation when you need to solve a problem.

3. **Product training experience** is your hands-on experience with a product or service under training conditions. Most technical training is constrained to a limited scenario that aligns with how the vendor thinks their product should be used. Real world deployments often stray from that ideal usage due to a wide range of factors that influence how we deploy technology in our unique organizations. There is still value in product training experience even if you haven't used a product in the real world yet. You can develop and maintain your training

experience by reading tutorials and training guides, watching or attending training courses, and sitting certification exams.

4. **Product usage experience** is your hands-on experience with a product or service in real world conditions. This is your 'on-the-job' experience and can be highly valuable as you learn how a product behaves outside of the vendor's ideal usage scenarios.

The best outcome is to put some time into all four areas of your skills. There will be ebbs and flows as you focus more on training one month, then implementation another month. But over the course of the year you should be satisfied that you're growing in all areas.

Soft skill development

Keeping your skills sharp doesn't just involve technical training, but also business and personal development. Soft skills such as business writing, leadership, and time management are important, no matter what role you're in. You develop soft skills in two ways:

- Learning from books, training courses, or observing others

- Regularly practicing and using the skills

This is an area of constant learning. You should be working on growing your soft skills each year just as you work on growing your technical skills. Fortunately there is a wealth of information out there to help you grow in these areas.

You can find a list of my recommended books and other resources at **survivingitbook.com/resources**. I will also cover the soft skills of people management and time management in more detail in Chapters 4 and 5.

Developing and Maintaining Skills

To stay employable in the ever-changing technology world you need to:

» Build a solid foundation of conceptual awareness. This must not be overlooked because it is the basis upon which all your more specific capability, product training, and product usage knowledge is built.

» Stay up to date with the capabilities of the leading and emerging products in your areas of interest.

» Undergo regular product training in some form, whether it be classroom training, online courses, books, free videos on YouTube, or reading vendor documentation.

» Use the products that are available to you to the maximum extent possible. Simplicity is good, but a lot of us barely scratch the surface of what's possible with the products we're using day to day.

BLOGGING AND SIDE PROJECTS

Your resume makes claims about what you know. You get a chance to back up those claims in job interviews. Other people in your personal network can also vouch for what you claim to know. But one of the best ways to *demonstrate* your skills is to have a public portfolio of work.

Think about it, if you were to hire a landscaper to help you with your garden, would you hire the one that has a bullet list of services and a phone number on their website? Or would you hire the one that has photos of other garden projects they've completed, and a YouTube channel sharing gardening tips?

Technology workers have it easy in many respects, because our skills can be easily demonstrated.

- **Blogging and article writing** shows that you can explain a concept or problem clearly and concisely.

- **Book writing** demonstrates that you have a depth of understanding on a topic, and have the persistence to complete the long and fairly tedious publishing process.

- **Publishing videos on YouTube** shows that you can present material in a confident manner and with high production quality.

- **Podcasting** demonstrates that you can hold conversations with other experts, draw out information in a useful way, and speak confidently on topics in your field.

- **Sharing code** demonstrates that you can write clean, useful scripts and tools that work when used by people of varying skill levels.

- **Any form of public content sharing** demonstrates your attention to detail, how you interact with other people, and respond to feedback.

I attribute much of my career success to my willingness to share content and knowledge publicly. I've blogged for over 12 years, participated daily in forums and online communities, ran a podcast for a few years, and have made most of my scripts and tools available to the public on GitHub.

That said, it can be a lot of work. In one year I published as many as 130 new blog articles, on top of my podcasting, book writing, and working on training videos. This volume of production worked for me because blogging, book writing, and training courses were becoming my primary source of income. Consulting and other client work had become a secondary activity for me.

I'm not recommending you follow my lead in terms of quantity if all you want is a good public portfolio to help with your career. If I were looking at blogging as a complement to my day job in IT I would only aim to publish one or two good articles per month. Combined with one or two scripts or tools that I maintained on GitHub, that would be enough to showcase my skills. A lot of the people you see today who are well known for their content started out that way, just running a simple blog or YouTube channel and letting it grow slowly to a level that felt comfortable for them.

For some recommendations on how to start your own side project go to **survivingitbook.com/resources**.

SOCIAL MEDIA, FORUMS AND COMMUNITIES

As you meet and get to know people in person, make a digital connection as well. For all its faults, LinkedIn is the de facto contact list for professionals these days. The day after you've met someone, go look them up on LinkedIn and send them a connection request. Personalize it with a simple note such as "Nice to meet you at the Product X meetup. Hope your upgrade goes well, maybe we can compare notes next time."

Facebook groups are also good places to maintain connections with people who you have things in common with, but don't want to invite into your personal life by adding them as a Facebook friend. Twitter has been popular over the years, and still is for some topics. Other communities have a stronger presence on sites like Reddit or on Slack channels. Find the ones that allow you to make meaningful connections with people, share your knowledge, and reach out to when you need help yourself.

Many years ago I spent a lot of time on one of Australia's more well known online forums, chatting about technical topics and other areas of interest. In those days the concept of a 'personal brand' wasn't widely discussed. It was normal for people to use nicknames and pseudonyms online instead of their real names. I was no different, operating under a nickname I'd acquired some years earlier.

What I found was people who were interacting behind a fake name tended to behave in ways they probably wouldn't if they were using their real name or speaking in person. I even fell into the trap myself, getting into arguments that were out of character for how I acted in real life. There's something about anonymity that brings out the worst in people. Or perhaps it brings out their real personality. That's a debate that could go on forever, and not one I want to get into (at least not without a nickname to hide behind ... get it?).

Despite my bad behavior in some discussions, I had generally built up a positive reputation. I enjoyed the conversations, sharing my knowledge and helping people with problems. I recognized other users on the forum, and they recognized me. The trouble was, I couldn't leverage that positive reputation to benefit my professional life. There was no connection between that forum persona and my real name. And if I established that connection, it would also connect my bad behavior on the forum to my real name.

The experience taught me two valuable lessons:

1. Don't say anything online that you wouldn't say to someone's face.

2. While anonymity is important, building a good reputation online that you can't leverage in real life is not a good investment of time.

I eventually abandoned that forum identity and started to establish myself online using my real name. Twitter, Reddit, other forums, Slack channels; all of them use my real name and photo. I take steps to protect my privacy and personal life, but I otherwise put myself out there in public and let people see the real me.

It hasn't always been perfect. I get frustrated at times and have let myself get drawn into arguments now and then. But for the most part I behave the same way online that I would in person. I write carefully, because I've seen how a hastily written post can come across as rude or abrasive.

In doing so, I've learned some important life skills.

One is to be more empathetic when writing comments. It's easy to criticize software bugs and use dismissive words like 'crap' and 'garbage' as descriptors. But that software I'm criticizing is someone's professional work, something they have poured time and effort into before sharing with the world. They know it's not perfect, but they're doing their best.

The other life skill is to preserve my energy. You don't need to look far to find something online to get angry about. There are conversations going on every day where you can barge in and add your opinion to the mix. And there are mistakes everywhere that you can point out to people. All of that takes energy. If you're wondering why you feel tired and unmotivated at the end of the day, it could be because you've spent all your mental energy arguing online.

PERSONAL FINANCES

If your career is a business that means you need to be financially stable to survive. Personal finance is a huge topic that is covered in a wide range of books, online courses, and other material. I'm not a personal finance expert, so I'm not going to give you specific advice. What I will say is that there are two things you should have if you want to avoid financial troubles.

The first is **basic financial literacy**. Understand how banking works, and how inflation impacts the value of your cash. Understand how credit cards and loans work, and the difference between good debt and bad debt. Understand how taxes work—especially how they impact your take home pay. And understand basic budgeting so that you can live within your means and not slide deeper and deeper into financial strife.

The second important thing is **understanding your financial position**. Things that affect this are your cash reserves, assets and investments, and retirement savings. Having lots of assets such as property might seem like a strong position. But if you have debts that exceed those assets, or you can't liquidate them quickly when you need emergency cash, then you might find yourself in trouble.

Your cash reserves are of particular importance when it comes to your career. Many of you are already familiar with the concept of a 'f*** you' fund. This is an amount of money you have in reserve in case of the need to quit your job on the spot. I would like to think you can avoid such a situation with some careful maneuvring around whatever problems you're facing at work. But I realize some people unavoidably find themselves in a situation where if they don't quit their job immediately it is going to cause them serious health problems, or even kill them.

I'm not a frugal person by any means. There is 'fat' in my budget that could be cut if needed. I have a gym membership, cable and Netflix subscriptions, a big download allowance on my internet connection, and many more small luxuries that all add up. In some ways this is a good thing. If we fall on hard times, there are obvious areas to make some quick cuts if we need to spend less money. In the meantime, life is for living.

Having disposable income now is no excuse for not learning useful life skills. We eat out sometimes, but we also know how to cook. If money was tight we wouldn't eat out. But some people would find themselves at a loss for how to feed themselves if they couldn't afford takeaways anymore.

Living a bare-bones lifestyle with no margin for error can be a stressful situation in itself. Being frugal and cost conscious is not the same as preventing yourself from enjoying life. If a Netflix subscription and a daily coffee brings you happiness, by all means keep them up. But not at the expense of your financial stability.

Quitting a job isn't the only situation where you might need some emergency cash to survive. Studies have found that the leading cause of bankruptcy in the USA is medical bills. Even in countries where the public health system protects people from facing such expenses, not being able to work due to illness can still break you financially.

Fortunately there are insurances available to cover those situations. And although I'm not qualified to give you specific advice, it is certainly worth investigating your options to get insurance cover for illness, loss of income, death, or permanent disability. There is some comfort to be had from knowing that if you become seriously ill, your family will not find themselves homeless when you can't make your mortgage payments.

In modern times we also have a lot of our most important information secured in online accounts. Ask yourself whether your family or friends would know what to do if you were incapacitated.

- Can they get to your passwords to deal with your accounts?
- Could they access your savings to ensure that your bills are paid?
- Could they sign contracts on your behalf to sell assets?
- Do they know where your will is stored?

Sort Out Your Personal Finance and Life Decisions

The hardest part of getting your life squared away is having to think about the worst possible scenario. It's hard. I know because I've been through it myself.

» Do a budget for yourself or your household. Work out how much is coming in, how much you're spending, and how much you need to be saving or investing. Be honest with yourself and include everything. Small expenses add up fast.

- » If you have unmanageable debt, e.g. you're paying interest only, deal with that immediately. Speak to an adviser if you need help creating a plan to get it paid off.

- » Look at your worst case scenarios. Think of it as disaster planning. What would you or your family do in each situation? Do you have savings or insurances to cover those scenarios?

- » Write up an emergency plan and store it in a fire safe or safe deposit box where the right people can get to it when they need to.

CHAPTER 3 RECAP

It's worth investing time and energy in building your network within the industry as many of the best roles are never advertised. Those that are advertised often go to the person with the personal connection at the company.

- Moving up the career ladder will almost always require you to leave the company you're currently with. The ability to do your current core duties at a consistently high level is key to being given opportunities to ascend that ladder.

- It is rare for an employer to invest in keeping your technical skills current. You will almost certainly have to do this for yourself and it need not cost a great deal of money.

- Soft skill development is as important as developing your technical skills—especially if you hope to take on a managerial position some time in the future.

- Blogging and other side projects are an excellent way to build a public portfolio and a personal brand that can be leveraged to progress in the industry.

- Personal finances are a crucial part of managing the Business of You. Poor financial management can force you into decisions that solve short-term financial problems at the expense of long-term career progression.

CHAPTER 4
DEALING WITH PEOPLE

There's no escaping it. IT is a people business. Technology does not exist for the sake of technology. Your work as an IT professional supports businesses that are made up of people. And it's true what they say about people; no two are exactly alike.

To survive in IT, your ability to understand a broad range of people and personalities will be as important, if not more important, than your ability to understand technology. To understand people the most important skill for you to have is empathy.

Empathy is the capacity to understand or feel what another person is experiencing from within their frame of reference.

In other words, it's your ability to put yourself in other people's shoes and see things from their perspective.

Empathy is what will allow you to understand what a person expects, wants, and needs from a situation. Whether you're fixing a broken printer, designing a new system, or making a sales proposal, it is empathy that will lead you to the outcome that the other person wants.

People are people, and they deserve to be treated as people. Your customer isn't a problem. Your boss isn't an asshole. Your co-worker isn't annoying. They are all people who have needs, just like you.

DEALING WITH MANAGERS (ESPECIALLY THE BAD ONES)

I've worked for some great managers in my career, people who taught me incredible business and life lessons. But I've also stuck it out with some less than ideal bosses because I liked the job I had.

Experience has taught me that even a bad boss can be fine to work for, if you apply your skill of empathy. Remember: empathy allows you to understand what a person expects, wants, and needs from a situation.

If your boss expects you at your desk by 8:30am and that is something you're willing to comply with, then why not just do it? Yes, we'd all prefer flexible hours and a boss who measures our performance on results instead of arrival time. But if the worst thing about your job is your boss wants you to be at your desk between certain hours, is that the hill you want to die on?

Maybe it is, and more power to you. Fight the good fight and show your boss that your performance has nothing to do with arbitrary desk hours. Or quit and find something more to your liking. But don't do it out of frustration and a lack of understanding of what your boss really wants. Your boss just expects you at your desk at 8:30am because it makes them feel that their team respects them, and they like knowing their team is on deck and dealing with the important work of the day by that time. If you can empathize with that, the insistence on arriving on time becomes far less annoying.

The same goes for sudden, urgent requests from your boss. If they tell you to generate a report of something by the end of the day when you're already super busy with something else, don't say yes. But don't say no either. Apply your skill of empathy to the situation. Here's an example.

> **Boss:** "I need a report of all email distribution lists that aren't being used anymore. And I need it by the end of the day."

You: "That's not one of our standard reports, so I'll need to look at how that can be done. May I ask first, what is the problem or decision that is behind this request? I want to be sure that the report I create is on target for what you need."

Boss: "The CEO has had complaints that there are too many lists to choose from and it makes it hard for people to find the right one to send to. She wants to get rid of any we don't use."

You: "Okay, I understand. Like I said, that's not a standard report, so I'll need to look into it first. I'm working on our ticket queue right now which has some jobs due today. Should I leave those while I look into this for you, or can you wait for an answer tomorrow?"

Boss: "All right, work on those tickets first then get me the answer tomorrow and I will go back to them."

Now, it's important that when you make a commitment that you honour that commitment. Your manager is answering to your customers, so when you promise your manager something, you've effectively promised your customers.

You: "I looked into the inactive email distribution lists. We don't have a report that answers that question, but there is some log data we could use to make a reasonable guess. It only goes back 30 days though, which is risky if we're talking about deleting the groups. I suggest we raise a ticket to develop a script to pull info from those

*logs for the next 90 days. Then we can look at the report
and submit change requests for approval to delete the
groups that look unused."*

Do you see how empathy helps you get to that point
in a conversation? To some people the request seems
like an annoyance. Who really cares if a few unused
distribution lists are visible in an address book? They
don't cost anything to sit there.

But that's not what your manager sees from their
perspective. Your manager:

- has been asked to solve a problem that the
  CEO has (people complaining)
- has committed to finding a solution to the
  CEO's problem
- wants to show the CEO that their team
  is reliable and can be counted on to solve
  problems

You've also demonstrated to your manager that you are
responsive to their needs, and are able to take a sensible
approach to achieving outcomes.

You might be thinking this seems fine in an example
like the above where a seemingly reasonable manager is
involved. But what if you have a manager who's constantly
bombarding you with low priority distractions and
unclear instructions. A manager who tends to ask for

specific actions, rather than explain desired outcomes. A manager who just expects you to 'work it out yourself' when conflicting priorities arise. Or a manager who over-promises and commits to deadlines without any care for what is realistic.

To me those are signs of a bad manager. A manager's role is not to say yes to everything and then pass the work to you, making it your problem to deal with. Good managers are protective of your time, help you to prioritize workloads, and align your work to real business needs.

If you've got a bad manager on your hands, for a job that you like and want to keep, use the following mental checklist to guide your interactions. Do not leave a conversation, or take ownership of work being passed to you, until you can answer these questions:

- **Who is asking for this?** Bad managers tend to have many 'great ideas' in their idle moments, and love to toss them at you to deal with. I call them 'idea grenades.' Knowing the difference between a customer/business request and a manager's idea grenade is important.

- **What is the outcome you're looking for?** Too often we're asked to take an action, rather than achieve an outcome. Many times the action you're asked to take will not be the right action to achieve the desired outcome.

- **What business benefit does this outcome achieve, or what business problem does it solve?** Many 'great ideas' have no actual worth to the business. It's important to understand why you're being asked to do something.

- **What in our current workload is this more important than?** Prioritizing work is crucial to avoid having the latest 'great idea' push aside all the other unfinished work. Your backlog of unfinished tasks will only get longer if the latest request is always treated as the most important.

- **Are all the other key people aware of this?** Most work doesn't happen in isolation. You'll need other people to play their part in achieving the desired outcome. But if other staff and teams aren't on board with what you're being asked to do, it can become a case of 'your problem is not my problem' when you try to get other people to help you.

- **When does this need to be completed?** Clear and realistic deadlines are important. So is flexibility. All deadlines are meaningless if work simply takes longer. If you need to push back on an arbitrary deadline, you need to do that up front and not at the last minute as you're about to miss the target.

Dealing with bad managers can be draining because you have to spend energy to manage a manager. But, that's still a better situation than letting burnout drain you of every scrap of enjoyment you have in your job.

It's also worth noting there are two types of bad managers.

The first are those whose management style you struggle with, but you get along fine with them as people.

The second are the ones who are just not nice people. They are the type who plot behind the scenes to gain advantage at your expense and who will throw you under the bus, blaming you for every customer problem.

What can you do if you have the second type of manager?

This is where I need to remind you that people don't leave bad companies, they leave bad bosses. You deserve to be treated well by your manager. And if they won't treat you well, there are better managers out there who deserve to have you on their team. Go find them.

BEING MANAGED

Being an IT professional means working as part of a team. You can be the smartest, most talented technology worker in the world, but if you aren't willing and able to work as part of a team—if you're unmanageable—you're not going to be successful in the long run.

There's a good chance you've worked with some unmanageable people in the past. Unmanageable people tend to:

- Always think they are right. They don't respect other people's opinions, and respond with negativity when others express their ideas and opinions.

- Be set in their ways and demonstrate unwillingness to learn new things or try new approaches. They have reached a place of comfort and complacency, and resist any attempts to push them outside those boundaries.

- Do their own thing, regardless of what the business or the team is trying to achieve.

- Reject criticism, and rarely admit they're wrong. There is always someone or something else to blame for their failings.

How do unmanageable people survive? I've observed two situations in which these people can maintain a career, and even thrive.

The first is when they operate in two modes. To their teammates they exhibit all the characteristics of an unmanageable person. But to their actual manager, they act completely different and mask their true characteristics. The manager may even think of them as a superstar, but be unaware of the toxic effect the person is having on their team.

The second is when they're promoted as a means of removing them from a position where they are doing harm. Unfortunately this often means moving them into low to mid-level manager roles. If you wonder where bad managers come from, they often come from bad team members.

You can't control how others behave. All you can do is focus on being manageable yourself. For the most part that means acting like a grownup and a professional.

- If you disagree with someone's opinion, you can have a constructive discussion about the pros and cons of your opinion versus theirs. But when the team, or your manager, comes to a decision about which way to proceed, be a professional and play your role in helping move forward.

- Avoid the temptation to say 'we've always done it this way.' Just because it's the way it's done today, that doesn't mean it's the best way in the future. New technology and capabilities come along that change how we do things all the time. Be open to trying new things and objectively evaluating them against the desired outcomes.

- Always ask yourself whether your actions are helping your team or your business move towards their goals. We can keep ourselves busy all day with work that ultimately achieves nothing of substance. When you strip away the unnecessary, you have more time to focus on what really matters.

- Accept criticism and own your mistakes. It will help you to grow in the long run.

Being manageable doesn't mean being a pushover. You still need to protect yourself from overwork. In Chapter 6 I go into personal health, and the important topic of burnout. You also need to protect yourself from abuse, and recognize when your growth as a professional is being stifled. If your ideas are good but never accepted by the team, it could be that you're being held back by someone else's ego. Likewise, if you're constantly being criticized but never praised, it could be that you're stuck in a culture of abusive behavior. Criticism comes from all directions sometimes, and it's hard to filter the good from the bad. That's why I have a simple rule: never accept criticism from someone who would never pay me a compliment.

DEALING WITH CUSTOMERS

It's often said that working in IT would be great if it weren't for the customers. But obviously, without the customers we wouldn't have a job in the first place. After all, we're there to provide a service to people, not play with technology all day.

And it's an unfortunate truth of the IT industry that, most of the time, we're meeting customers at their worst. If there's ever a time where empathy is needed, this is it.

When something is broken, the customer can't do what they need to do. When you're the person responsible for fixing it, it's important to disengage from how they are acting and remember they mostly want to know three things:

- that you understand their problem
- that you understand why it is important to them
- that you're going to solve their problem for them.

If that's what they want, give it to them. It goes a long way to calming them down and getting them on your side. Play your cards right and they'll be raving about you afterwards too.

Start by acknowledging the information they've already given you (because nobody likes repeating themselves) and then ask them to confirm it is correct.

> "I have your support ticket here. It says you're seeing an error when you try to book meetings for your manager. Is that still correct?"

If they confirm that the problem statement is correct, set the scene for what is going to happen next.

> "This is a new problem and we don't have any information about why it's happening. So what I'd like to do if it's okay with you, is have you repeat the steps you were going through while I observe, and perhaps I will see a clue for what is causing the error."

If you can't see any solutions right away, and it's likely you will need to go and research the problem, reassure them that you understand why this problem is important to them.

> "Okay, I can see that this is going to cause you problems as you try to manage your boss's calendar, so we need to get this fixed for you as quickly as possible."

Then set expectations for how you're going to proceed from here. But be cautious about over-committing to something you aren't sure you can achieve.

"I'm going to try and reproduce the problem here and see if there's a fix available. I will give you a call back within the hour to give you a progress update if I haven't found a solution sooner."

Nothing will shatter a customer's good impression of you more than not following through on a promise. If you've done the hard work to get the customer on your side and believing in you, only to disappoint them by not staying true to your word, the relationship with that customer will be damaged. But if you earn a reputation as someone who is honest and who follows up when promised, that will go a long way to keeping customers happy with you, even when you don't always have the answers they need.

If you can't solve a problem yourself, say so. Let the customer know you've spent some time on it and can't find a solution. Next you're going to escalate to a colleague or a higher level of support, or if necessary, open a support ticket with the vendor. Again, keeping the customer updated and managing their expectations will go a long way to keeping them happy. They don't like being unable to work, but they'd rather be informed than uninformed.

Customers see technology as an enabler, or as an obstacle, depending on how well the technology is working that day. And to many customers, technology is a great mystery. This is becoming less of an issue as new generations grow up using technology earlier in their lives. But a large portion of the workforce still struggles with technology today. It's a source of stress and frustration. They don't want to understand it. They just want to do their job. So if you can get technology out of their way, make it as invisible and seamless as possible, you'll make their work a lot easier.

One of the common complaints by IT professionals is that their customers don't listen to them when it comes to changes and upgrades for their systems. We often attribute this reluctance to the customer being cheap. IT is an expense, and most business owners try to keep expenses low, therefore technology spending is limited.

I can't say that I blame the customer. If you own a car, and the car has a few problems that annoy you, it's not an automatic solution to replace the car with a new one. Sure, the new car will have few, if any, problems and will be covered by a warranty. It might also have some new features that make your driving experience more enjoyable. But it's still a big expense to buy a new car. In your mind you will evaluate the trade-off. Is it worth all that extra money to solve a few minor problems with your car? If it's doing the job, even to a minimum level of satisfaction, then every day you don't replace it is a day you've got that money available for other things.

It's not until the car completely breaks down that the decision becomes easier. And that's exactly how our customers think as well. What works today is good enough. The best salesperson in the world won't overcome that point of view.

Another common problem IT professionals have with their customers is that many customers remain reluctant to change. This has an unfortunate side effect in that, when they eventually do concede that an upgrade or replacement of some part of their IT is important, such a long period of time has passed that the users experience a feeling of shock at just how different the new system is. Because they've skipped all the incremental changes over the years, they find themselves being hit with something so different, it pushes them way outside their comfort zone.

While we're often excited to take a customer from their old system to the latest solution, from the customer's perspective, especially the end user, it's highly disruptive. Understanding this will help you manage the customer's needs and reactions better.

In the end, it's important to remember that customers are people just like you. Use empathy, treat them well, and they will treat you well in return.

HOW TO ASK GOOD QUESTIONS

You don't know everything, and you never will. At some point you will need to ask people for help. Either you will ask your colleagues, or you will ask the public on a forum or discussion channel.

There are no stupid questions. And even 'easy' questions are fine. I know I don't mind answering easy questions because it's a fairly low energy thing to do.

What very few people can tolerate is poorly asked questions. Especially poorly asked questions from a person who never asks good questions. Everyone has a bad day now and then, and asks a bad question. But those who do it repeatedly will find themselves irritating the very people they need help from.

So how do you avoid asking bad questions? Or rather, how do you ensure you are asking a good question?

To begin with, you should always seek to find answers yourself. When faced with a new problem you should:

- validate the scope of the problem
- search your internal knowledge base for a solution
- search the internet for a solution

- refer to documentation for clues as to why the problem is occurring

- attempt to reproduce the problem in a way that reveals a solution

Each of those steps is important, because you will often solve the problem yourself. But when you don't, you will have a solid basis for asking a good question when you seek help from others. You will already know:

- the scope of the problem (i.e. who is impacted, and how)

- whether there is an answer in your internal knowledge base or on the internet (i.e. is the problem well known)

- whether the documentation explains why the problem is occurring (e.g. if you are running a configuration outside of recommended practices)

- whether the problem can be easily reproduced

This is all crucial information to take with you when asking others for help.

Consider a simple scenario of a user experiencing an error when they try to print documents. Imagine the help desk member going to a server engineer and asking this question:

"John says he can't print. Is there a problem with printing at the moment?"

The engineer is not going to be happy about being interrupted with a question like that. The help desk member has not brought any of the information that would be useful to the engineer, such as whether:

- John can print other documents, print from other applications, or print to other printers
- the error message John is receiving, if any, is found in the knowledge base or on the internet with a suggested fix
- the printer settings match what is in the documentation
- John's nearby colleagues have the same problem when they try to print

In contrast, if the help desk member has followed the steps outlined above, they could ask a good question.

"John says he can't print. He gets an error 57 message when he tries to print any document from any application. He tried another printer on a different floor and it worked. I tried printing to the same printer and I get the same error. I checked for previous tickets like this and couldn't find any that match. There were some old forum posts I found in Google that suggested some changes to a printer setting, but ours is already set that way. I have those links if you'd like to read them yourself. I can't find any obvious differences between the printers that work and the printer that doesn't work. Can you suggest what I should try next?"

I don't know too many people who would be unhappy being asked a question that way. In that situation myself I would happily respond with a few suggestions or, if none spring to mind, agree that the help desk should pass the support ticket over to my team to look into it further.

The last step in asking good questions is to close the loop. When you've received the correct answer, acknowledge it. Let that person know that the information they provided was what led you to the solution. If there's more details to share, or if you found the solution yourself, share that knowledge as well. Add it to the notes of the support ticket. Update your internal Wiki. Send an email to your team. Or, if you've asked for help on a public forum, write a comment with the solution for others to find later when they stumble across your thread in a Google search.

Asking Good Questions

Nobody can work in complete isolation. At some stage you are going to need the help of others to solve a problem. That means that your ability to ask good questions is an essential skill in your career as an IT professional. Here are some pointers to keep in mind:

» Describe the goal or outcome that you are trying to achieve. Asking people to tell you why a command is failing is not a good question if you haven't explained what the end goal is that you're working on.

» Describe the environment that you are encountering the problem in, such as operating systems, virtualization platforms, versions of software, whether you are remote or local to the problem, and what your role is in the scenario (e.g. end user, support technician, project manager).

» Use simple language, short sentences, short paragraphs, and check your spelling for errors. People will struggle to help you if your question is hard to read.

» Provide specifics, such as error log entries, but prune them to the relevant portions. Expecting someone to read 200 lines of error logs looking for a one-line error is not being respectful of their time.

» Be polite, receptive to suggestions, and respectful of people's time that they are giving you for free.

HOW TO BE A GOOD TEAM PLAYER

In basketball, a team is made up of players of many shapes and sizes. From the tallest center to the shortest guard, each player brings a unique set of skills and strengths to the game. Some players are great shooters but weak defenders. Some are tall and powerful, but slow. Playing together as a team they can win the game.

In IT we sometimes find that people expect all team members to be equal in skills. If you have four 'server engineers' all getting paid roughly the same salary, is it fair that one of them doesn't know how to troubleshoot a clustered SQL server?

Actually yes, that is fair. Because that team member who doesn't know about SQL clusters just happens to be great at dealing with Citrix farms.

In a team, everyone contributes to a common goal. That shared goal is only achieved when teams are made up of complementary skill sets. Instead of having identical technical skills, what we really want from team members are common personality traits. And I don't mean that everyone on the team loves Star Wars or football. I mean that they all share the same qualities:

A committed 'buy in' to the team's goal

Teams work best when they are working towards a common goal. If you feel your goals are not aligned with the rest of the team, take some time to consider why that is. Do you disagree with the goals of the business? Do you have an ethical problem? Or are you just more interested in doing something else?

A focus on solutions rather than problems

When people focus on finding someone or something to blame for a problem, they take time and attention away from solutions. Teams work best when they focus on solving technology and business problems, instead of finding excuses and scapegoats.

A willingness to take on challenges outside their comfort zone

Although everyone in a team brings different skills to the table, nobody should stay boxed in to a limited skillset. Teams grow in value and effectiveness when everyone is willing to step up and tackle new problems that they've never seen before.

Reliability and a willingness to take ownership

Teams work well when members can rely on each other to be responsible for the tasks they have been allocated. Team members also need to rely on each other to take ownership of new problems that they discover, and not ignore them or leave them for others to find.

A willingness to help their teammates

Teams are not made up of individuals working in isolation from each other. They are working towards a common goal. So if a team member needs your help, as a good teammate you will help them. Whether that's by spending time with them, directing them towards other resources, or by taking on other tasks to free up time for them. The team can't succeed if each team member is only focused on their own individual success.

Respect for each other's differences

Everyone in a team is a unique individual. Diverse teams are stronger and more effective, because they bring a wider range of life experiences and perspectives to the table. As a team member you must respect and value the differences in your teammates.

The ability to listen to others

Every person in a team has value to add. In discussions, don't just listen for your turn to speak. Actively listen to what others are saying, acknowledge them, and give them the consideration that they deserve. They may be right, and they may be wrong. But then so might you.

The ability to communicate openly and honestly

Teams need to trust each other to share information. Knowledge-hoarding by individuals will weaken a team's effectiveness. Furthermore, each team member must be confident that others are being honest and upfront with them in all matters.

CHAPTER 4 RECAP

- Not all managers are good. Not all bad managers are bad people. If you have a career in IT, it's almost guaranteed that one day you'll have to manage a bad manager.

- Empathy—the ability to see and understand other people's points of view, motivations and situations—is key to being able to manage bad managers. It's also key to effectively managing customers.

- Ask good questions. Good questions provide the person you are seeking help from with all the key information they need, and demonstrate you have tried to help yourself first. Asking good questions will greatly endear you to colleagues, superiors and people in online forums. They will also make people more willing to help you.

- When you work in IT, you will be part of a team. One key to having a long and successful career in IT is being a good teammate. Part of being a good teammate is being someone who is good to manage.

- Being a good team player also requires you to exhibit:
  - 'buy in' to the team's goals

- a focus on solutions rather than problems
- a willingness to take on challenges
- a willingness to take ownership of problems you encounter
- an understanding that everyone is different and those differences should be respected
- an ability to listen to others
- an ability to communicate openly and honestly

CHAPTER 5
PRODUCTIVITY

If you're like me, when someone approaches you with a question or a problem, your instinct is to help them. You want to give them an answer or a solution. And you want to give it to them fast because doing so makes you feel productive. Since you like feeling productive, you keep helping people with their 'quick and easy' problems.

Before you know it, you're the go-to person for everyone's quick and easy problems. And you're caught in a trap. The helpfulness trap.

But wait, it gets worse.

You're now so addicted to the buzz you get from helping people, if they come to you with something that doesn't have a quick and easy answer, you utter these four words:

Leave it with me.

Now you're in a situation where not only are you solving other people's 'quick and easy' problems for them in the moment, you're holding on to other people's more difficult problems. Problems you don't fully understand.

This is where you start feeling overwhelmed. There's too much work to do, and too many people needing your time and attention. You owe people answers. And it feels like you're so busy solving everyone else's problems there's no time to solve your own.

The end result?

Your days become filled with *other people's work*. Work that has little to no meaningful purpose to you. This disconnects you from what motivates you and causes you to become disengaged at work. As the cycle continues (because you haven't done anything to stop it), new problems are piled on your plate which creates stress, anxiety and frustration. Before you know it, you're completely burnt out.

So what can you do differently? How do you avoid this vicious cycle? Is it as simple as saying no when people ask for help?

No, it isn't, because, in the IT industry, we are in the business of solving problems.

The real solution requires you to change your habits. Specifically, you need to develop a coaching habit.

DEVELOPING A COACHING HABIT

Athletes have coaches. Sports teams have coaches. Business owners often have coaches too. But if we're not planning to coach athletes, sports teams, or business owners, why do we need to develop a coaching habit?

In his book, *The Coaching Habit*, author Michael Bungay Stanier writes:

> "The essence of coaching lies in helping others and unlocking their potential."

We are all coaches, whether we realize it or not. A teammate coming to you for help is a coaching opportunity. A customer coming to you with a problem is often a coaching opportunity as well. Even your boss coming to you with a task is sometimes a coaching opportunity.

By viewing each of those scenarios as a coaching opportunity, you can help others to increase their self-sufficiency. This enables them to do more without you. This will both reduce your workload, and remove you as a bottleneck in the system. It will also free up more time for you to work on things that matter, which will increase your level of motivation and engagement. You'll find yourself doing less work, but having a greater impact.

When people like you develop a coaching habit, it solves the problems of over-dependency, overwhelm, and burnout.

So where do we start? As Bungay Stanier puts it:

> "A little more asking people questions and a little less telling people what to do."

When presented with a problem, instead of jumping in with solutions, Bungay Stanier offers these seven questions to ask first:

1. What's on your mind?
2. And what else?
3. What's the real challenge here for you?
4. What do you want?
5. How can I help?
6. If you're saying yes to this, what are you saying no to?
7. What was most useful for you?

Before we break down what the above can look like in real life, let's examine a typical situation.

Your teammate Jeff comes to you with a problem.

> "Bob from Finance says the daily reports aren't showing up on time."

Your instinct is to be helpful and solve the problem. The database server is probably running slow. "Leave it with me," you say to Jeff. And off he goes, content that Bob's problem is now yours to deal with.

See how easily you've fallen into the helpfulness trap? You're already busy, and not only did Jeff interrupt the work you were doing to share Bob's problem with you, Jeff has now removed Bob's problem from his plate and put it on yours. And you've got no real idea of the scope of the problem, what the root cause is, or what the priority is for getting it solved. It could be anything from a minor complaint by Bob, to a full blown crisis with millions of dollars at stake. And if your first hunch (the database server running slow) turns out to be wrong, you're going to have to keep working to find the solution.

Let's look at the same situation, but apply Bungay Stanier's coaching questions:

Jeff: "I need your help with a problem."

You: "What's on your mind?"

Jeff: "Bob from Finance says the daily reports aren't showing up on time."

You: "Okay. And what else?"

Jeff: "He says it's been a problem for a few weeks now." (Ah-ha! It's not a sudden crisis.)

You: "I see. And what else?"

Jeff: "Well, I've checked the database server, and it seems to be running fine. I'm not sure what to do next." (Ah-ha! Jeff has already checked the most obvious cause.)

You: "Good, I would have checked the server performance as well. I can think of a few other ideas, but what else do you think might be causing the problem?"

Jeff: "I guess the schedule might be set to start too late."

You: "I agree. And what else might be possible?"

Jeff: "Maybe the report itself has a problem."

You: "That's possible too. So what's the real challenge here?"

Jeff: "I can change the report schedule, but I don't know how to fix the reports if that is the problem. I don't know enough about them."

You: "What do you want to do?"

Jeff: "Well, I'll try setting the report schedule to run earlier. But if that doesn't work someone will need to look closer at the reports."

You: "Sounds good. And how can I help?"

Jeff: "Can you look at the reports to see if they have a problem?"

[This is where you need to ask yourself, if I say yes to this, what am I saying no to?]

You: "No, I can't. I'm working on the firewall project for the rest of this week. Tell Bob that if the schedule change doesn't fix his problem, you'll put a job in the system to have the reports checked next week at the earliest. If he needs it done sooner, he will need to approve a contractor to come in and help with it."

Jeff: "Okay, I'll do that."

You: "Great. So, what was most useful for you?"

Jeff: "Well, it's good to know that checking the server performance was the right idea. And that we can adjust the report schedules if we need to. I also didn't realize we could get outside contractors in to help with this kind of problem."

As Bungay Stanier writes in The Coaching Habit:

> "The goal here [of these questions] isn't to avoid ever providing an answer. But it is to get better at having people find their own answers."

If you're a person with skills and knowledge, or the responsibility to deal with certain tasks, then people will come to you for help. This is inescapable.

Running through the seven questions removes the knee-jerk 'leave it with me' response that leads to overwhelm and burnout. It ensures that if you end up saying 'yes' to helping someone with something, you're doing it more slowly and mindfully. And that only the work you should be doing ends up on your plate.

Because the reality is, we can't always say no. There are many situations where saying yes is the only possible outcome. That could be because there is nobody else who can solve the problem. Or because a customer is paying you to do it. Or because your boss is making it non-negotiable. And that's okay, because those situations where yes is the only answer will have more time to be dealt with if you've offloaded the other meaningless work from your plate.

The seven questions ensure we only accept responsibility for a problem once we have a better grasp of the situation. This helps us to avoid overcommitment that comes from agreeing to impossible deadlines.

They key is to not be a robot about it:

- add some warmth to your voice
- show interest in the person's problem and their answers to your questions
- vary your questions, but don't stray far from the formula

I would encourage you to skip the small talk, and get to the first question promptly.

> **Jeff:** *"Hey, how's it going today?"*
>
> **You:** *"Good thanks. What's on your mind?"*

From there, you can progress in a friendly way. Notice in the example earlier I wasn't simply repeating the "And what else?" question over and over. Instead, I acknowledged their answers before asking the next question. "I see. And what else?"

If your fear is that you'll become known as The One Who Always Asks Those Questions, ask yourself this: Is that a worse outcome than being overwhelmed with other people's jobs and getting burned out?

Besides, Bungay Stanier thinks there's a good chance your fears are unfounded.

> "... most likely you can think of someone in your organization who seems to be able to 'hold the line' and stop that aggregation of small tasks and additional responsibilities that, for the rest of us, eventually consume our lives. That person might not be the best-liked person in the organization ... but they're likely to be successful, senior and respected. And that's because they know how to say yes more slowly than you do."

Developing good coaching habits reduces your problem load, and stops you from becoming a bottleneck for others. And ultimately that helps everyone, not just you.

TAMING EMAIL

A lot of people think email is broken. They get too much email, most of it is rubbish, and they dread looking at it. Often they feel that email is more harmful than helpful to their productivity. Opening email is a chore.

Email alternatives are plentiful today. Slack, Microsoft Teams, WhatsApp, Facebook Messenger … there are many non-email methods of communicating. Sometimes they're an improvement, other times not. You can become overwhelmed by Slack messages as easily as you can email messages. Bad communication habits are bad habits, no matter which app or medium they're applied to.

Email isn't broken for everyone, but it might be broken for you. I'm not a raving fan of email myself. My job is not to read emails. Reading more email doesn't earn me more money. With few exceptions, reading email doesn't bring me more joy. The more time I spend on email, the less time I'm spending on my business and things that make me happy.

Email is a necessary function. But it only provides me with personal or business value when used correctly. To me that means:

- receiving fewer emails
- spending as little time dealing with email as possible

We recently moved our business to a new office. As anyone who has moved offices will tell you, there are a thousand little things to do for an office move. Our move took months of planning, culminating in a furious week of packing up the office. Moving day started with a 4am wake-up for me. And although we managed to get the new office opening and functional by lunchtime, it still took part of the weekend to finish setting things up.

I barely touched a computer in that final week of the move, and only triaged email on my phone for a few minutes each day. Usually when you take someone away from their computer and their normal duties, they return to a huge pile of unread emails.

Not me. It took me less than 30 minutes to 'catch up.' Then I got back to work.

I'm not writing this to brag. Rather, I want to share with you how I got to the point where a week of disruption didn't leave me with a mountain of unread emails to deal with. My days are not spent dealing with my inbox. Email is a task that takes up less than an hour of my time each day, in total. And that's on a busy day.

It didn't happen overnight. In fact it took me about a year of steady progress to get to this point. Here are my best tips based on that progression:

1. Minimize email volume

The most obvious solution to reduce the time you spend on email is to receive less of it. To receive fewer emails, you must:

Answer questions before they're asked

Give your users self-service options for repetitive requests. Give your support staff documentation so they don't need to reach out to you. Put a FAQ on your website. Not everyone will use it, but you'll cut down the number of emails you receive by a lot.

Unsubscribe what you aren't consuming

Get rid of the newsletters you aren't reading. If you haven't read one in a few months, it's obviously not that important to you. If you do need to keep up with industry news, subscribe to just one or two high quality, curated emails instead of dozens of individual sources. The most important information will bubble to the surface anyway. Everything else you can seek on Google or by asking peers when you actually need it.

Switch off what you don't need

Email alerts and notifications are often a waste of time. Working in support and operations roles, I didn't need to know that a Priority 2 or 3 ticket had been assigned to me. I will see it when I go to my ticket queue for my next task. The associated email notification is unnecessary. Even Priority 1 tickets don't need an email since they were also alerted by SMS/text and a phone call. The same goes for other notifications, such as social networks. I check LinkedIn for a few minutes a couple of days per week. I check Facebook in the evenings or during short breaks during the day. I see the notifications in the app, so there's no value in receiving notifications in my inbox all day as well.

Feed work straight into work queues

Most businesses have a customer service email, or a sales form on a website, or something that generates email. Send those items straight into the workflows that they belong in, and cut out the manual handling.

Kill long email chains

If your email conversation is bouncing back and forth without a conclusion, pick up the phone and solve it that way. Or schedule a short meeting with the right people to come to an agreement.

Separate work from fun

This may seem like common sense, but keep your personal life out of your work mailbox. A personal email address with Gmail or Outlook.com is free, has good security with 2FA, and has decent spam filtering.

Send fewer emails

Yes, you're part of the problem too.

What's left over should be mostly email that is necessary. There might still be a lot of it. That means it's important to be able to process email efficiently.

2. Process email efficiently

It's often said that email is a great way for other people to inject their priorities into your day. This is true, and one of the main reasons is that we tend to sort our email in order of newest to oldest. Whoever has emailed us most recently becomes the top item in the inbox. This is why annoying marketers send frequent follow up emails. They want to reclaim the top position in your inbox.

Because we're conditioned to think that all email is important and deserving of a prompt and thoughtful reply, we allow ourselves to give the most visible emails all our attention.

The problem then becomes that the oldest tasks are pushed so far down your inbox by the new emails that keep arriving, they lose any chance of being actioned. Out of sight, out of mind.

Sort email from oldest to newest

This is why my first piece of advice for improving your email processing efficiency is to sort your inbox the other way around—in order of oldest to newest. Unless some other signal tells you that a more recent email is more important, deal with your oldest items first.

If that creates an unacceptable delay in you getting through all the email you're receiving, you're receiving too much email. Either go back to my earlier advice about reducing the amount of email you receive, or keep reading and try and process your email more efficiently.

Sorting email from oldest to newest solves the issue of older items being overlooked. But it doesn't make your inbox any better at being a to-do list. In fact, your inbox is the worst place to store your outstanding tasks. There's no sense of priority, urgency, due dates, time spent, status, or anything else that goes with effective task management.

Action quick replies/tasks immediately

Don't leave tasks sitting in your mailbox, waiting for you to 'get back to it later.' Especially tasks that you can't complete immediately. If something is a quick reply or two minute job, go ahead and do it right away. You've already interrupted some other work to check your email, so you may as well finish actioning the quick messages immediately.

Move time-consuming tasks out of your inbox

If something needs a longer reply or will take longer to work on, get it out of your mailbox and into your task management system. Don't hang on to that email for Bob's reporting request that you need to start working on next week. Add it to your tasks/to-do system so that it pops up on your list on the appropriate time and day. Then archive the email away where it won't distract you any further.

That might sound strange, but it's how I handle emails that need some time to consider and reply. After reading the email once I will create a to-do item such as 'Respond to Julie's email about database updates,' and set it to pop up on my task list for an appropriate time in the future. I'll either attach the email message to it (if the system supports it), or just archive it away and search for it again when the time comes. No stress of needing to remember to get back to that email.

Use filtering

Very little of my email arrives into my inbox. Most of it is filtered by a series of rules that moves messages into folders. For example:

- automatic notifications for things like backup jobs completing go into a separate folder (failures stay in my inbox)

- newsletters go into one of two folders (one for business newsletters, one for technical newsletters)

- emails that I am cc'd on go to their own folder

- emails that I have received as a member of a distribution list go to their own folder (a few DLs have earned their own dedicated folder, but most get pooled together)

Use the archive function

I'm not one who likes a complex mailbox folder system. Aside from the messages that I filter above, all my other email goes to my inbox. When I process it, I archive it. Outlook has an 'Archive' button that just moves messages to an 'Archive' folder. Gmail has a similar archive function that has the same effect.

No need to think about where the email needs to go. Just archive it. If I need it later, I can search for the person's name or a few keywords and find it in seconds.

3. Process email in batches

So you've minimized your email volume and aggressively filtered your inbox. What's left in your inbox now needs to be dealt with. And I've found batching to be the most effective way to do this.

Each morning when I sit at my computer I process the emails that have arrived overnight. I start with the emails that have been filtered into folders. Customer service and sales emails are a priority, so they go first. After that I spend a few minutes checking system notifications for anything unusual.

Then I look at my inbox. Inevitably something unwanted will have arrived, which I either delete if it's the first time I've seen it, or unsubscribe if it's a recurring nuisance. You've got to nip these things in the bud.

If I still have a few minutes left I deal with other messages, but when my allocated batch processing time is up, my calendar will remind me that it's time to get down to the real work for that morning.

I don't look at my email again until shortly before lunchtime, and then one more time near the end of the day. Often those batch sessions are just quick triage of other email that doesn't need a response, such as flicking through my distribution list emails on my phone while waiting for my coffee.

Decision overload is a problem in modern life. The mental burden of decision making wears us down a little bit at a time. I remove the burden of deciding what's for dinner by meal planning the entire week in advance. I remove the burden of deciding when to exercise by having specific days and times for workouts. I remove many other decision-making burdens from my life in similar ways.

When I batch process my email I want to deal with it then and there. The last thing I want to do is rush through all my email and mentally load myself up with a bunch of decisions that I need to remember for later. Quick emails get actioned immediately, and the rest goes into my task list. When time runs out, the rest waits for my next batch window.

Again, if that leaves too many emails untouched until tomorrow, or too many tasks in your queue than you can deal with in a week, then the problem might be that too much work is coming in to begin with. There's only so much optimization you can do before it's time to hire more people to handle the workload.

Do what works for you

You might have noticed elements of different productivity systems in my way of doing things. In the past I've given a surface look at GTD (Getting Things Done), Inbox Zero, personal Kanban, and various others that escape me right now. Some are general productivity systems, while others are targeted at email.

Whatever I've taken from those systems and made my own is mostly subconscious, and in some cases probably just a coincidence. To me that's the best way to approach productivity. Take a little bit from here and a little bit from there, and merge them together into a system that works for you.

That's why I don't recommend one specific system. What makes sense for you will be different to what makes sense to others.

Some of you might be reading this and thinking that my advice doesn't apply to you. Perhaps you feel it's unrealistic for you to reduce email, or process it differently.

I no longer work a typical IT job. I'm self-employed and a business owner, but I still answer to others. I have customers, staff, other businesses I've partnered with, suppliers, and more. People email me wanting things, and I have to deal with those emails just like you do. More importantly, my staff have to deal with email as well. I don't want them to be overwhelmed and unproductive because of email.

And, most importantly, my methods for dealing with email worked just as well in my last job as an IT consultant as they do today in my role as a manager. The advice works for many situations if you are consistent in applying it.

For example, if people are emailing you support requests directly instead of going to your help desk, don't respond to them. If you respond, you create an expectation that you are responsive to emails. That invites more emails. Instead, carry on with your high value work, and leave the email until your next batch processing window. If it's a quick answer, deal with it once. If it's a more complicated request, add it to your task list or ticket system and let it wait its turn (first in, first out).

Email gives you something to react to. When you are receiving too much email, there's always something there in your inbox to spend time on. You can check your email in much the same way someone checks Facebook or Twitter—to distract you from the sense of needing to do something else. Email becomes the ultimate procrastination tool. It sucks up time and relieves you of the need to deal with things that actually need your attention.

Without email to react to, you need to make harder decisions like "what should I work on next?" The good news is, you can focus your attention on deep work. It takes some getting used to, but the habit becomes easier once you've created the space for real work to take place. Instead of sitting down and opening email to see what your next task is, you can sit down and plan out a productive day. Then once your morning email processing is complete, spend time on high value work that moves you, your job, or your business forward.

PRIORITIZING TASKS

I don't like the term 'ASAP.' Nothing about ASAP tells me what I really need to know about prioritizing a task or request. Is it urgent? Is it important? Or does the person just want it done 'as soon as possible' for their own personal satisfaction.

If you ask people whether their requests are urgent or important, they'll tell you the request is both of those things. It probably is urgent to them, possibly because they procrastinated and now they're up against a deadline of their own. And I'm sure it's also important, because whatever they're asking you for directly impacts their job. (Remember, most people you deal with in IT as customers and end users are focused solely on their own priorities.)

Some of us in IT are fortunate enough to work in organisations with clear SLAs in place. SLAs are an agreement between a provider and a customer, whether that is an internal or external customer, describing how a service is provided. It will cover things like availability of services, expected response and resolution times for requests, and consequences for not meeting those targets.

In some ways, SLAs are easy to work with. A medium-priority request must be resolved in 24 hours. A high-priority request must be resolved in four hours. The SLAs define what is medium priority, and what is high priority. In theory this means you simply work on tasks in order of due date. In practice, however, it's not always that easy. Mostly because SLAs are often poorly defined, and customers self-select the priority based on their own subjective views rather than genuine business impact.

When everything is urgent, nothing is urgent.

The other issue is that most SLAs don't control how much work is generated by a customer. So excess workload is a problem that isn't solved by an SLA. You would think that an SLA would actually make it easier to deal with excess workloads. If SLA targets are not being met, a provider knows they should hire more staff to support that customer. Right? Sadly this is not the case. Decision-makers seem to like dealing with the problem by telling their staff to 'work smarter,' which is code for "We don't want to spend more money on staff, so instead we're going to imply that you're just not working to your maximum potential."

Working smarter is a nice idea. But how exactly do we do it?

If I gave you a list of ten tasks to complete, and only enough time to complete five of them, how would you deal with that? You can't work hard enough to get them all done, so you need to work smarter. Would you tackle the oldest items on the list first? The new items? Or perhaps you'd do the smallest, easiest ones first, and hope there's time left over for the big stuff.

Prioritizing tasks is key to getting your workload under control, especially when you have a backlog that you're struggling to deal with. A helpful exercise is to assess all of your work against two metrics:

1. Impact for the business (or customer)
2. Effort to complete

Using those two metrics, each piece of work that you are responsible for will fit into one of four categories:

1. **High impact/low effort** - these are quick wins that you should prioritize in the short term as they carry long term benefits.

2. **High impact/high effort** - these are major projects that should be scoped in detail and have resources dedicated to them.

3. **Low impact/low effort** - these are small, routine housekeeping tasks that should be delegated or automated.

4. **Low impact/high effort** - these are tasks that are wasting more time than they're worth and should either be delegated, automated, or discontinued entirely.

As a matrix it looks like this.

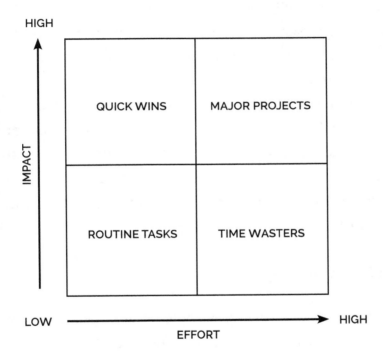

Sit down with a piece of paper and draw lines to divide it into four quadrants. As you look through your work, categorize each item into one of the quadrants. You'll quickly see what you should prioritize in the short term, what needs resourcing for longer term effort, and what you should seek to delegate, automate, or get rid of completely.

You can apply the same categorization to new work that comes in as well. Whether you're overloaded or not, new work should be assessed for impact and effort. If someone comes to you with a request or an idea for a project, run it through the matrix. This will immediately tell you whether the work has genuine benefits (impact), and whether it can be implemented as a quick win or needs proper scoping and resourcing. You'll also immediately see when ideas are just change for the sake of change. Different is not always better. If a proposed piece of work is going to be high effort for low impact, it's probably not worth pursuing in the first place. The matrix helps prevent unnecessary work from being added to your workload, which helps you avoid overwork.

AUTOMATION

Automation is a polarizing topic because people think that automation will replace their job. Automation can't replace your job, it can only replace tasks that you perform.

When you automate replaceable tasks it frees up time for you to perform higher value tasks. It's only when your entire skillset is made up of replaceable tasks that you have a problem.

Rather than seeing automation as your enemy, you're better off seeing it as a reminder that your career must be built on valuable skills. Avoiding automation won't help you. In fact, embracing automation is more likely to help you in this situation, because you will develop the skills to automate replaceable tasks, support those automated processes, and solve more of the problems your business has. Now that's a highly valuable skill.

When talking about automation at a company level, I've found conversations tend to focus in an overly simplistic way on its time-saving and cost-saving benefits. While saving time and money are certainly two *potential* benefits of automation, they are not the *only* driving factors.

Here's a more nuanced approach you can bring to the automation conversation the next time it comes up in your company.

Automation drives quality

This is because you can't automate a process you don't understand. Completing a process accurately every time drives consistency because automation doesn't get lazy and skip steps to save time. And automation never forgets how a process is performed, even if it hasn't recently run that process.

Automation is more easily scalable

To scale up a manual process you need to hire and train more people. To scale up an automated process you simply add more computing resources.

Automation allows you to be more agile

When a manual process changes, everyone who uses that process needs to know about the change. That takes time and communication, and it's easy for someone who is not paying attention to slip back into the old way of doing things, or simply forget that the process has changed. Automated processes can be changed rapidly by updating the script or code that runs.

Yes, automation saves time

But first you have to invest time upfront to automate a process. And then it will take time to reap the time-saving benefits. This is where I think many IT professionals miscalculate. It's also important to note that not every automated process needs to save you large amounts of time. Automating a series of ten different five minute tasks saves you very little on a task-by-task basis. But you will save 50 minutes of time in total. Probably more when you take into account the time lost when switching from one task to another.

Automation also saves you time on repeat processes, or reruns. Here's an example:

On one customer project I needed to migrate 200 web pages from one platform to another. A manual copy-paste of the page would have taken half the day to do. Instead, I spent that half-day writing a script to migrate the web pages automatically. When the time came to run the migration it only took a few minutes to complete. So, no time saving yet. But, sure enough, the next day the customer told me that several of the pages had changed on the old server and needed to be re-migrated. Instead of spending time hunting down which ones had changed, I simply reran the script and the changes were migrated across in minutes.

Automation is a simple solution, but not an easy one

To turn a manual process into an automated process you must:

1. Learn an automation tool or language (such as Python or PowerShell).

2. Understand the process, its dependencies, and any conditions that might cause it to branch off in a different direction.

3. Write the code or implement the tools to automate the process.

4. Monitor and debug the automation until it is running reliably.

And that's just for one process. Granted, you can reuse your learnings in Python or PowerShell and apply them to multiple automation scenarios. But there'll still be unique elements of each problem that need you to invest time to learn how to solve them.

MAKING PEACE WITH INCREMENTAL PROGRESS

Working in IT means facing big problems every day. Some of those problems need solving in order to make your working life more enjoyable. For example, if you're swamped by work involving repetitive, manual processing, the obvious solution is to start automating that work.

Big problems are made up of smaller problems to solve. If you only focus on the big problems, it can be quite daunting. It can feel like any progress you make is meaningless until you have solved the big problem in its entirety. This can be a serious productivity killer.

This is why it's important to break big problems down into small problems. Each small problem you solve is a victory you can celebrate, one that takes you incrementally closer to your goal. In the automation scenario I mentioned earlier, the big problem is that you're doing too much manual processing of routine tasks. It's going to take time to get to a point where 90% or more of your manual processes are automated. This big goal can be broken into smaller goals, such as:

- **Goal #1**—identify the top ten manual processes that are taking up your time.

- **Goal #2**—spend 30 days learning the fundamentals of PowerShell.

- **Goal #3**—write a PowerShell script that handles one of the top ten manual processes.

- **Goal #4**—improve the script to the point where you feel comfortable handing it over to your team to use. Or, even better, that you feel comfortable having the script run automatically to handle those tasks.

That's progress you can build on. Once you get that first process automated, you can take what you've learned and automate the next process after it.

The same approach can be used for any big problem you're facing. Give yourself a fighting chance by breaking it down into small, manageable chunks, and then start to make incremental progress.

DEALING WITH INTERRUPTIONS

A technology professional's day usually consists of three types of work:

1. **Proactive, routine processes**
   (e.g. daily backup checks, monthly reports)

2. **Reactive support tasks**
   (e.g. responding to tech support calls, alarms)

3. **Innovation and improvements**
   (e.g. developing new systems, upgrades)

Different technology roles will spend different portions of their day on those tasks. A help desk worker will spend more time reacting to support requests. A tier 2/3 system administrator will tend to have extra responsibilities to innovate and improve systems.

Striking the right balance is a challenge in overworked, understaffed teams. There is a natural tendency to deal with the problems that look like fires. Work is a never-ending stream of 'urgent' requests. But that leaves no time for innovation and improvement. We have to make time for it.

I say 'make' time, because there isn't a bunch of spare time hidden away somewhere that you can 'find.' You have to remove other things from your day to make time for the work that is most important.

The biggest obstacle is that we work in environments of frequent interruption.

- **Reactive support work** is immune to interruption. The urgency of reactive work allows us to say no to interruptions that are less important. If something more important does come up, we can return to a problem and refocus fast.

- **Proactive, routine process work** is also immune to interruption. It is simple to return to a routine process and pick up at the last step you were working on.

- **Innovation and improvement work** is different. This work requires extended periods of deep concentration. But sitting and thinking about a challenging question can look and feel unproductive. This makes innovative work especially prone to interruption. The coworker who sees you sitting still will assume you're not busy, and will interrupt you with a question. The manager who measures output through perceived effort instead of actual results, will assume you need more work to do.

Many studies have measured the impact that interruption has on productivity. The accepted wisdom is that interruptions don't only consume time for the duration of the interruption itself. They can also impact your mental progress for up to 30 minutes after. When a five-minute chat becomes a 35-minute loss of productivity, you can see the problem.

As time passes and interruptions continue, the problem spreads even further. Work piles up. Stress levels rise. Our moods and general well-being deteriorate. Productivity declines as we start to resent the interruptions that keep us from making real progress. Burnout is a common outcome of this type of work environment.

A career in technology involves working on complex systems. And technology moves fast, so things also change rapidly. We need to learn complex things quickly, then adapt as they change.

When was the last time you were able to quickly learn a complicated new technology while being constantly interrupted? I would think the answer is 'not recently.' But it's important to keep learning otherwise you risk becoming a commodity worker in an industry that places little value on such skills.

And it's not enough to learn new skills. You also need to create value. Unfortunately, value is not created through repetitive, process-driven, reactive work. Value comes from innovation and improvement. In other words:

- the type of work most vulnerable to interruptions

- the type of work that requires extended periods of focus and concentration.

The way most people find those extended periods for focus is by working longer hours. (When everyone else has gone home, there's finally peace and quiet to work on a challenging problem.) Or they work from home in the evenings and on weekends.

I've done this myself, to varying degrees of success. A few nights or a weekend spent bashing out a problem that saves me an hour a day is worthwhile. But spending every night and weekend doing work is neither worthwhile or healthy.

To make space for focussed work in a healthy and sustainable way, we need to remove distraction and interruption. On a personal level, the solutions are well known. Cut down on social media, close your email, and turn off smartphone notifications. I take Facebook, Twitter, and Reddit completely off my phone for most of the year. Facebook gets reinstalled only when we're traveling so I can keep up with friends while on vacation. Twitter only gets installed if I'm at an event or conference that is using it as a primary social channel.

Likewise, with emails, texts, and phone calls, I have my phone set to automatically enable *Do Not Disturb* mode at 6pm each evening. Only my wife and a few family and friends are able to interrupt me after that time. I might unlock my phone and check for messages now and then, but that's an active decision on my part and not an interruption. This has allowed me to spend my evenings giving full attention to my family, or a personal project that I'm working on, or even just reading a book without my phone trying to get my attention.

In a professional setting, it gets trickier. How do you turn off interruptions yet still do your job? How do you dedicate blocks of time to focussed work when anyone can walk up to you with a question or a five-minute chat?

One simple trick is to work with a teammate. Working with someone is the ultimate cure for interruptions and distractions. People are less likely to interrupt you when you're already with someone. It also keeps you focussed on the task at hand and removes the temptation to check email or quickly browse Reddit.

A more complex solution that needs some management support is to block out big chunks of your day where you:

- can't be booked for meetings
- don't answer phone calls, and
- don't accept walk-up interruptions.

That last one is tricky if your office doesn't have a way to prevent people from walking up to you. I've seen teams go to the extent of hanging a sign at the entrance to their area that says the team is unavailable between certain hours of the day. If someone believes their problem is important enough to interrupt them, they are requested to call the team leader who will filter those requests and pull aside a team member when necessary. That was a difficult change to implement, and it ruffled a few feathers in the organization, but eventually things calmed down and productivity improved.

The most important thing is that you're consistent with your boundaries and expectations. If you're known as someone who doesn't respond to email straight away, but who always replies by the end of the day, people will get used to that and accept it. If you're known as someone who is available for meetings in the morning, but not the afternoons, people will get used to that too. And if you're someone who politely turns away interruptions that aren't emergencies, directing people to use email or your ticketing system instead, people will get used to that and stop bothering you with unimportant matters.

MULTITASKING

Multitasking is a myth. Much as we'd like to believe it, we really can't work on more than one thing at a time. When we think we're multitasking, what we're actually doing is task switching.

Yes, even when you think you're multitasking by running a process on one screen, and reading your email in another screen while you wait for the process to finish, that's really just task switching.

Every time we switch tasks, we lose time. Our brain has to stop one activity, then start another one. Task switching is a self-created interruption. At a micro level, these interruptions may only cause a few seconds of lost time. But they also drain our energy and increase the chance of making a mistake.

Over the course of several hours, constantly interrupting yourself to switch tasks costs you time, energy, and accuracy. Give your tasks the focus they need.

MEETINGS

The majority of meetings in the workplace are a pointless waste of time. And time is money. As I once saw posted on Twitter, you aren't trusted to authorize a $500 purchase but you can call an hour long meeting for 20 people and nobody cares.

I once worked in a distributed team of about ten staff with two managers. Each week we held a team meeting via conference call for an hour. The meeting always lasted an hour, and provided very little real value to the team. The team leader opened the meeting by sharing various news and announcements. Rarely was there any discussion about the announcements. The only constraint on the team leader was to leave enough time for the rest of the agenda items.

After 30 to 40 minutes of information sharing the team leader would finish speaking and then we would 'go around the room,' each person sharing a brief update with the team about their work and any current issues they were dealing with. With eight to ten team members sharing their status update in just 20 minutes of meeting time we all became quite adept at summarizing our points into one to two minutes. The meeting would then wrap up at the one hour mark as planned, and we'd all get back to work.

Personally I found this meeting to largely be a waste of time. To prove this, I decided to flip things around. Each week a different team member took turns chairing the meeting and keeping notes. When it was my turn, I changed the normal order of speaking and started with everyone's quick status updates. After 15 minutes everyone had shared what they wanted to share, and I turned the meeting over to the team leader. This put him in an awkward position. If he spoke until the end of the hour, it would seem he was just speaking to fill the time. Instead, he spoke until he'd shared all of his important matters, and then stopped. We wrapped up the meeting in just 30 minutes instead of the usual hour, a total saving across the team of five hours of productivity.

Meetings have a way of expanding to fill the allotted time. That team meeting was a perfect example. Worse, the meeting was multipurpose, which actually diminished its usefulness rather than enhancing it.

If you search online for 'types of meetings' you'll find many different results telling you there are anywhere from five to 16 types of business meetings. In my view there are only three types of meetings worth having:

1. status meetings
2. decision meetings
3. workshop meetings

Most of the other meeting types you'll see online can be grouped into those three types. Some are not really meetings at all. For example a sales meeting, (whether you're 'selling' to a customer or to your managers to go away afterwards and make a decision), is really a presentation or an event, depending on the scale.

Each of the three meeting types achieves a specific goal:

1. **Status meetings** are for sharing information of any size
2. **Decision meetings** are for making decisions or coming to an agreement
3. **Workshop meetings** are for developing ideas or solving problems

Any meeting that attempts to combine two or more of those goals is a bad meeting. A status meeting that gets sidetracked into debating a decision, or goes down a rabbit hole of problem solving, will inevitably be wasting the time of several attendees who are only there for the main purpose of the meeting.

And in a lot of cases, the same goals can be achieved without holding a meeting at all.

Status updates can be provided via other channels such as email, chat/IM software, and project management systems. This works particularly well in distributed teams and staggered shifts. Why wait for the entire team to arrive in the morning before sharing status updates? The early starters can share theirs then get to work, while the later arrivals can come in and read what's already shared, then add their status update as well.

Decisions can be reached by asking for suggestions then running a poll to select a way forward that most people agree with. Even better, choose just a few key people to make a decision instead of giving everyone a say in the matter. It's nice for everyone to have a voice, but not every decision needs everyone's input. For example, pick two people to select the monitoring products to evaluate instead of asking the entire team of ten. If they get stuck then they can solicit some more opinions from others. By shrinking the number of decision makers they become more invested in the process, develop a greater sense of responsibility and ownership, and aren't just throwing in a vote to go along with everyone else. Pick a different two people to decide how to plan a system upgrade, a different two people to choose a new report template, and so on. Everyone gets to make decisions, but not everyone has to be involved in every decision.

If you must hold a **decision meeting** for something big and important, give each attendee all of the background information so they can review it beforehand. Explain the problem, the desired outcome, and the pros and cons of each option for moving forward. The goal is for everyone to come to the meeting ready to reach an agreement on the decision. If they aren't prepared, they don't get a say in the decision. A few questions or clarifications are fine, but don't get sucked into workshopping the issue or re-explaining it to someone. If you haven't provided enough information for a decision to be made, end the meeting, go away and try again. Few people like to make an important decision under time pressure, so you shouldn't expect ill-informed meeting attendees to have to decide based on last-minute information.

Workshop meetings can be quite valuable if done correctly. Workshops should be as isolated and distraction-free as possible to ensure everyone is focussed on the problem at hand. They should also be shorter than you think they need to be. A full day workshop sounds like a great way to innovate on new ideas. But energy levels tend to wane later in the day. Instead, try a series of shorter workshop meetings with space in between them for people's idle minds to chew on problems. You might just find that planting a few seeds in people's minds on a Tuesday morning will yield better ideas on Thursday than if you just sat in a room for an entire day thinking about the matter.

More Effective Meetings

As a **meeting organizer** you should always know what the goal of your meeting is, and respect people's time.

» Always clearly state the purpose of the meeting and provide an agenda.

» Replace as many status meetings as you can with check-ins instead.

» Schedule meetings for the minimum possible time. A ten minute meeting from 2:05pm to 2:15pm lets people know that they are showing up for a quick, deliberate matter and not a 30 minute or longer chit chat.

» Use standing areas for meetings. A meeting room with no chairs is perfect for this. Otherwise, implement a 'no sitting' rule. Standing up ensures people don't get relaxed and comfortable as this can lead to distraction and 'waffling on.'

» Start on time, always. If someone is late don't make everyone wait while you stop to catch them up.

» Don't 'go around the room.' If you're seeking input, ask one person, then ask a second person if they agree or disagree. If the question can't be resolved that way then a separate decision meeting should be scheduled so you can move on with the purpose of the meeting you're already in.

» Always record and send meeting minutes to attendees along with agreed decisions or action items (ideally these go straight into your task management system).

» If someone is only needed for part of a longer meeting, let them know that they can come late or leave early.

» Cancel meetings that aren't providing value. If a weekly project status meeting is wasting time because the project is moving slower than expected, or because status updates are being well-communicated via other channels, then there's no need to keep holding the meeting.

As a **meeting attendee** you can use the points above to set your own expectations of whether to attend meetings you're invited to.

» Decline meetings with no agenda or that have no clear purpose.

» Show up on time and keep the small talk to a minimum so the meeting can get underway on time.

» If you are no longer needed in a meeting, excuse yourself and leave. Why stay the full hour if the relevant portion for you was all finished in the first ten minutes?

» Block out parts of your calendar where you don't want to be invited to meetings. For example, keep your regular lunch break blocked out, and the last 30 minutes of the day so that you can wrap up your work and get out on time to catch the train home.

CHAPTER 5 RECAP

- Don't get stuck in the helpfulness trap. Develop a coaching habit to slow down the rate at which you say 'yes' to things, and to ensure the tasks you end up with are the tasks most appropriate for you.

- To ensure your inbox isn't ruling your life, you need to minimize email volume, process your emails efficiently (using filtering, sorting and archiving) and process your email in batches (at set times during the day).

- Use the impact vs effort matrix to effectively prioritize tasks and ensure you don't spend any time on high effort, low impact tasks.

- Don't look at automation as a threat to your job. Look at it as a timely warning to upskill (if your skill set is made up of replaceable tasks).

- Break big tasks and goals into smaller tasks and goals to keep your motivation levels up.

- Devise methods for reducing the number of times you are interrupted during the day as interruptions are the enemy of deep work.

- Multitasking is a myth. All multitasking is actually task switching, and task switching is a guaranteed productivity killer.

- Remember that meetings are giant productivity killers so do what you can to:

  - reduce the number of meetings in your life

  - make the meetings you are part of more effective.

CHAPTER 6
PERSONAL HEALTH

In Chapter 5 we looked at productivity. While it's true that you can use productivity tools and techniques to work more efficiently and effectively, there is no magic productivity hack that will solve an excessive workload. Even the most efficient system won't work if there is too much input for the available resources to process. If you have optimized your productivity and still genuinely have an excessive workload that doesn't fit into a reasonable amount of daily work hours, then it's important that you recognize the problem upfront before it develops into burnout.

You might be reading this and feel that while you're working longer hours to manage your workload, it isn't burning you out. I'm not talking about a sprint to deal with a short term spike in work. Those times will come along now and then. As will those times where a colleague falls ill and is away for a few days. Or someone quits, and there's a brief gap before their replacement is able to start working for you. Those situations are fine, as long as they are exceptions.

Problems arise when the exceptions become the rule and you find yourself lurching from crisis to crisis, in a chronically short-staffed state, with constant promises of things getting better 'once you get over this latest hurdle.'

Stress is good, in reasonable amounts and with adequate rest to compensate for it. Periods of manageable stress, followed by rest, are how we achieve growth.

But we simply can't handle extended periods of overwork without suffering a negative consequence. We do not have infinite capacity in us to work harder to compensate for overload. Persistent stress does not lead to growth, it leads to burnout.

BURNOUT

Burnout is a very real problem in the technology industry. Ironically, denial of burnout is one of the symptoms of burnout. People who are starting to burn out usually don't realize it, until they end up physically and emotionally crashing.

There are many signs of burnout. Some are more obvious than others. Most signs of burnout can be summarized into a few general categories. They are:

- poor life/work balance
- negative attitude
- declining mental health
- declining physical health

The main trigger for burnout is workload. Too many tasks, with not enough time to complete them, and no support or resources to achieve what is expected of you. Sadly, much of the technology industry accepts excessive workload as the norm. Martyrdom is commonplace, with workers sacrificing their personal time to work longer hours for no additional compensation.

Burnout is not always an obvious condition. When we think of burnout, we often think of someone 'snapping' or 'hitting the wall.' That type of total physical and emotional breakdown does happen. But for those people, burnout started well before they reached that point.

A negative attitude is one of the early signs of burnout. Most people will start a new job with enthusiasm and joy. That lasts anywhere from a few weeks to several months. Eventually the reality of a job sets in. Stress starts to accumulate. Little things about the job start to annoy you. Questions or problems are approached with a cynical attitude.

This doesn't happen at every job. Some companies have successfully solved most of the problems within their control that lead to employee burnout. But it happens at enough companies that I know many of you are nodding your head as you read this.

The negativity begins to degrade our mental health. Normal responsibilities start to seem like a chore. The prospect of more work starts to drain us of energy. Instead of feeling excited about new challenges, we dread them. That feeling can spill over into our personal lives as well. It's hard to wake up in the morning and feel unhappy at the prospect of another day at a job you don't enjoy, and not have that unhappiness manifest itself at home. Some people just go quiet, others become irritable and snappy with family and friends. Similarly, coming home from work feeling stressed out and exhausted leaves us no energy to spend that valuable time on hobbies or with loved ones. The mental rest and regeneration that we need, and that our hobbies and idle time provide, is no longer taking place. Without realizing it, a lot of people on the verge of a breakdown just feel miserable all the time.

Self-doubt creeps in as we start to question whether we're cut out for this type of career at all. Feelings of meaningless, and a desire to just quit, are often internalized because of workplace cultures that don't encourage open communication about stress and mental health.

The physical symptoms also creep up on us slowly. Weight gain, recurring illnesses, loss of fitness, headaches, fatigue, inability to sleep, and other physical symptoms are often triggered by burnout, but don't appear all at once. Unfortunately, they also contribute to a vicious cycle. When we're overloaded at work, it's common to spend more time working and less time taking care of ourselves. Without adequate sleep, we're less prepared to tackle the next day's challenges, which increases the feeling of overwhelm. And as stress leads to compensation with things like fast food and alcohol, our bodies start to take an even bigger battering.

Too many people these days embrace a 'hustle and grind' mentality. If you just work hard enough, you'll get on top of everything. And if you aren't there yet, then you must work even harder to get there.

But that's not the nature of IT work. Our job is an endless stream of new work coming in. You're never finished. All you can do is keep the work moving through at an acceptable rate. Pick up a new task, do it well, and close it off with no lingering bits left over to worry about. Draw a line at the end of the day and go home, satisfied that you've had a productive day. Enjoy your personal time, get some rest, and come back refreshed the next day to take on the next challenge.

Tips for Dealing with Burnout

Hopefully you recognize the signs of burnout before they become a serious issue for you. Stopping the problems before they become harmful is a lot easier than recovering from a breakdown. Sadly, many of us will get to that point at least once in our careers before we learn the lessons. To stop burnout in its tracks, here are some tips.

> » **Keep your work hours at a sensible level.** 40 hours is reasonable for a full-time employee. Unplanned excess hours should be rare. Planned excess hours should also be uncommon, and should be compensated by overtime or paid time off.

> » **Take breaks during the day.** I try to take a rest pause at least once per hour. Go for a short walk, use the restroom, drink some water, then work out what you're going to focus on next and go back to work. This is

also good for undoing some of the damage that a desk-bound job does to our bodies.

» **Take your meal break.** In a normal work day a 30 to 60 minute break is crucial. Get away from your desk and eat some food. Don't take calls or check emails. Ask your boss or teammates to text you if something critical comes up.

» **Take sick days when you're sick.** I consider presenteeism to be one of the worst habits of office workers. If you're sick, don't spread that around the office. Don't drag it out longer by continuing to exert yourself. Rest at home for a day or two and come back healthy. Work remotely if you feel able to. But you'll recover much faster and return to productivity sooner by resting.

» **Take holidays and short vacations throughout the year.** My family plans for a weekend getaway three to four times per year. You don't need to go far, just somewhere that breaks up the routine and provides some physical and mental refreshment. At least once per year we also take a longer vacation of a week or more. This can be as simple as a week away in a cabin by the beach, but we also enjoy saving up for overseas holidays every few years.

» **Treat your personal time as sacred.** Spend time with family and friends, being fully present with them and not distracted by work. Take up hobbies that are fun and give you energy. Use your free time to eat healthy and have an active lifestyle.

LIFE-WORK BALANCE

I don't like the term 'work-life balance.' I think it is a backward way of looking at things. A good life is more important than your work. Yes, some people love their jobs, and are passionate about their work. I love helping people solve problems. But I won't sacrifice my entire life to do it.

Having a life is crucial to avoiding burnout and maintaining your health and happiness. But a good life-work balance won't simply be handed to you. You need to fight for it, and once you have it, you need to defend it.

Andrew was a network administrator at a mid-sized company. He was the only person who could make changes to the network firewalls. The head of IT wasn't willing to pay to hire or train someone else to help

Andrew, so all firewall change requests needed Andrew to do the work.

With many projects ongoing at any time, there was a steady stream of firewall changes being requested. On top of his daily workload, Andrew was being asked to design firewall changes based on a project's requirements, get the changes approved through the change management process, and then perform the change.

Of course, you wouldn't want to make too many changes to a firewall at once. One change to the firewall configuration was permitted each day. The company was risk averse, and all firewall changes had to be performed outside of core business hours. Each change also needed to be tested, usually the next day. If the change didn't work, Andrew had to try again the next night.

Andrew's job soon became an endless backlog of firewall change requests, working each night to implement changes, and then reshuffling the backlog any time one of the changes didn't work. Andrew was constantly fatigued, getting home late each night after his kids were already asleep, and often working a few hours on weekends as well. The stress was piling up, and Andrew couldn't see a way out of it.

"What if you just say no?"

That was my advice to Andrew. Just say no.

I have worked for managed service providers (MSPs). Anyone who has worked for an MSP knows the workload is ridiculous, and expectations are that you will work 50+ hours a week so you can bill at least 40 hours on client work, if not more. Burnout is very common for MSP employees. I suffered from it myself. On one outrageously underestimated project I stayed awake for 37 hours straight, until I simply could not stand up. It was unsafe, but I didn't know any better at the time, and the project managers only cared about getting the work done.

After burning out from MSP work, I later found myself working for a mining company. Mining companies take employee safety very seriously, because mine sites are dangerous places. The same focus on safety extends all the way to employees in office buildings. Offices are a lot safer to work in than mine sites, but still have a surprising number of hazards.

The first thing I noticed was noone worked excessive hours. I was contracted to work a minimum of 36 hours per week and if I got all my work done in that time, I could call it a week. Meanwhile, the maximum hours I was allowed to work in a week was capped at 50 to prevent fatigue.

When I later joined an operations team at the company, the same focus on health and safety continued. If a teammate was up late dealing with an on call alarm, they simply messaged the team to let everyone know they'd be in late the next day so they could get some rest. Skills were shared among the team, so that no single person had to manage the entire load of a particular type of work. And if you had an evening change planned, you were encouraged to leave work early to make up for it.

That company taught me a lot about healthy workloads. The quality of my work increased because I wasn't tired all the time. When work requests came my way, I was free to say no and propose a different target date that wouldn't require me to work excessive hours. My moods improved to an almost zen-like state of calm, even when critical incidents occurred. I made better decisions and enjoyed the feeling that work would end each day, and resume the next, without the constant pressure to squeeze in more billable hours. I was home on time for family dinner more often than not, and always knew which weekends I was responsible for on call so that we could plan around it.

Which is why I told Andrew to just say no.

Now, obviously Andrew couldn't just refuse to do any work. He was responsible for making firewall changes, and those changes were critical for the projects that were happening. He needed a strategy to manage his workload while still keeping project managers happy.

But nobody else was going to solve this problem for him.

Andrew went to his manager with a proposal.

- All firewall changes for projects must be made on Tuesdays and Thursdays. No other days. This would allow Andrew to get his other work done without as many interruptions by projects.

- Andrew must be provided with the change details seven days ahead of the change window to allow him time to complete the change management process, which involved a weekly meeting of the change approval board.

- The project must supply someone to perform testing at the time of the change, so that any problems could be identified and fixed immediately instead of having to reschedule the change for another night.

- To make up for the two evenings of firewall changes, Andrew could leave the office early on Fridays.

Andrew's manager agreed to try it, but said that if it caused any project delays they would have to go back to the old way of doing things.

When I caught up with Andrew a few months later he gave me an update. At first, the project managers didn't like the new policy. They felt that it would slow down their projects. Andrew assured them that their requests just needed to be submitted about two weeks before they needed them, which was reasonable considering these projects were designed and planned months in advance. And by testing the changes immediately, they would cut down on the number of failed changes that needed to be retried later.

And it worked. Andrew felt (and looked) much better. The firewall changes were getting done, and Andrew was spending less time at the office in the evenings. He told me his family life now worked around his two planned evenings of work. Simple pleasures like reading books and watching Netflix were back in his life. On Fridays he was able to leave the office early and pick up his kids from school, and on weekends they could plan fun activities to do together as a family.

By not letting work consume his entire life, Andrew achieved a healthy life-work balance. And all it took was one small change to how he handled project requests.

If that sounds like an impossible outcome to you, I would ask you to really think about what changes you can make in your work that would make it possible. Remember, nobody is going to solve this problem for you. Come up with a plan that keeps your boss and your customers happy, and that gives you back control of your life.

If your plan is rejected, at least you tried. And now you can think seriously about whether it's time to move on and find a new job.

YOUR PHYSICAL HEALTH

I was 30 years old when our first child was born. Having a child puts a lot of things in your life into perspective. My mind was racing as I held our son in my arms for the first time. Suddenly we had a whole new set of responsibilities, me as a father, and my wife as a mother. I wanted to help provide a good life for our son. I wanted to play a role in his life for as long as possible. I've always enjoyed life and had reasons to live, but now I had a reason to live for a long time.

The biggest risk to me living a long life was my physical health. The last time I had weighed myself the scales read 115kg (that's 253lbs for you imperials). For a male of my height, that put me in the obese category of the BMI chart.

You know what's really hard to do? Look at yourself in the mirror and for the first time realize you're obese. Not stocky, big boned, or barrel chested. Obese.

It was no mystery how I'd become obese. My eating habits were terrible. I consumed too many calories each day, and a lot of them came from takeaway food, beer, and other junk. And my exercise habits had declined to the point where I wasn't even walking the short distance from my house to the train station each day, preferring to drive because it was a bit hilly and I didn't want to get sweaty.

Being overweight puts us at a high risk of a range of health problems including heart disease, kidney problems, high blood pressure, stroke, and diabetes. Excess weight puts pressure on our vital organs and joints, causes sleep disorders, and can lead to chronic health conditions that severely diminish the quality and duration of our life.

Being overweight wasn't just a risk to my health. It was also having a negative impact on my career. To put it simply, the fatter I got, the less confident I became. Going to a new customer site used to be one of the parts of the job I enjoyed, but now I felt a sense of dread at how people would judge me when we first met. Standing in front of an audience to deliver a presentation became a nightmare. My energy levels were low, causing my motivation to decline, and I was starting to have trouble delivering good quality results on time for my projects.

I even started to notice the avoidance habits I'd picked up, like waving off a crowded elevator because I didn't want to be that fat guy that squeezed in last and made everyone else uncomfortable.

I decided to make a change in my life. I'd made that decision before, tried to change for the better, and failed. This time I had a big reason to succeed—our son. I joined a gym near the office and started working out every day. I hired a personal trainer, told her I wanted to get healthy for my son, and gave her permission to push me harder than any other client she had.

Not all personal trainers are good. Some of them take their clients through the motions, knowing that most of them will quit in a few weeks anyway. Some of them take a deep interest in their clients, build a strong personal connection, and help their clients succeed in their goals. My personal trainer was one of the latter. She was the first one to tell me, "You can't outrun your fork." What that means is, no amount of exercise will overcome a bad diet. She laid out a plan for me. I would see her one session a week, work out on my own three to four other days each week, and log all my exercise and food in a small notebook. This was before the days of smartphones and health apps like MyFitnessPal. We had to do it the hard way, with pen and paper. Each week she would review my notebook and give me advice on where to make adjustments.

THE IMPORTANCE OF EATING RIGHT

Have you ever logged your eating and drinking for a week to see what it looks like? If you haven't, I highly recommend it. When I started keeping a food diary for my personal trainer, I realized just how much bad food I was eating. When you're tired, busy and stressed, it's easy to grab a burger and a Coke from the local takeaway for lunch, scoff it down fast, and get back to work. When you have to write 'burger, chips, and Coke' in a diary and show that to your personal trainer, it's a lot harder.

Most people fail at changing their eating habits because they screw it up, badly. Before I had a personal trainer to offer nutritional advice I'd made dozens of attempts to establish a healthy diet myself. They usually went something like this:

- **Saturday**, after a rough week and a big night out, I'd decide to change things.

- On **Sunday** I'd do my weekly grocery shop and buy 'healthy' foods.

- On **Monday** morning I'd eat a breakfast of eggs and fruit juice. I'd pack a chicken salad and take it to work with me. By lunchtime I'd be starving and wolf down the chicken salad in no time. I'd drink water all day, avoiding sodas and other sugary drinks. At home in the evening I'd cook up a chicken breast, make a salad, and eat it for dinner. I'd then fight the sugar cravings until bedtime, and go to sleep hungry.

- On **Wednesday**, having suffered through two whole days of this plan, my willpower would crack and I'd grab a muffin for morning tea. By mid-afternoon, with my energy levels cratering, it'd be off to the snack machine for a packet of chips or a candy bar.

- By **Friday** night, no surprises, I'd be ordering pizza for dinner and after eating it, push the whole idea of getting healthy out of my mind. You can't feel guilty about failing if you just pretend you never tried in the first place.

Naturally the first week of my food diary was embarrassingly bad. But my trainer was expecting that, and had a lot of great advice to give me. The first thing she told me to do was eat eggs for breakfast. I've already tried that, I told her. I get hungry a few hours later. Besides, it gets boring.

Of course, she had an answer for that. Add some extra egg whites to boost the amount of protein. Add a piece of wholemeal toast (no butter) for some slow release carbs. And use things like tabasco sauce, curry powder, or some cracked pepper to add flavor. Change it up day to day and you won't get bored, she told me. Besides, most people are happy to eat the same breakfast cereal every single day. The problem is, they're addicted to all the sugar and processed carbs, so they're willing to keep eating it. Health foods need a bit of dressing up sometimes to keep them from getting boring, because they don't always give us the same dopamine kick that highly processed foods do.

She then told me to try to eat something every two to three hours to keep the cravings from overcoming my willpower. A morning snack of some fruit or veggie sticks with cottage cheese, wholemeal crackers with some cheese, or a protein shake if I was short on time.

Lunch was where the magic happened. My trainer gave me a simple formula for creating lunches. A portion of lean protein, a portion of complex carbohydrates, and a portion of mostly green vegetables. Each portion was to be about the size of the palm of my hand. For protein I used chicken breast or lean beef. I simply cooked up a batch of it at the start of the week with some spices, and portioned out what I needed each day. For carbs I used brown rice and wholemeal pasta. And for vegetables I used those little bags of frozen veggies you can steam in the microwave. Because of the variety that was available I almost never ate the same meal twice in a week.

Throw in one more afternoon snack some days, and dinner that followed a similar formula to lunch, and before I knew it the weight started to fall off me. I kept track of my weight milestones in the food and exercise diary, and after a few months I proudly handed it to my trainer at the start of a session and pointed to the weight on the page—97kg (213lbs). I had lost 18kg (nearly 40lbs). She didn't let me celebrate for long. The session that day was brutal.

These days there is so much information available online for how to lose weight, it's hard to know where to begin. Ask around and you'll get all kinds of advice. Try a whole foods diet, plant-based, Paleo, vegan, Keto, low-carb, no-carb, no sugar, intermittent fasting. Install this app, track your macros, read this book, sign up for that program, eat these bars, drink these shakes.

It's crazy. And a lot of it is unnecessarily complicated. When my trainer moved away to a different city I kept going at it alone. I did more research into workout routines, macronutrient ratios, and zeroed in on habits and routines that worked well for me. A year after I had started, my weight loss had exceeded 30kg (66lbs) by following a simple system. You might have read about this system online as CICO—Calories In, Calories Out.

- Work out your daily calorie intake for maintaining weight.
- Track your eating and drinking (calories in).
- Burn more energy than you consume (calories out).

- Keep a balanced macronutrient intake of around 40% protein, 20-30% carbs, and 20-30% healthy fats.

That was enough for someone like me (who was obese) to start losing weight. Once you get some momentum going, you can then dive into more nutritional detail such as cutting out refined carbs and sugars, and eating a diet that is made up of mostly unprocessed foods you prepare yourself. Some of that will just happen naturally as you make adjustments to stay within the boundaries of that simple system. For example, reducing your carb intake will have you cutting down the amount of breakfast cereal you eat. But in doing so, you'll realize just how small a single serving of most cereals is, and you'll likely end up hungry an hour later. Instead, you'll go looking for alternatives that are more filling, give you better energy throughout the morning, and don't blow your entire daily carb budget on a single meal.

The rest you will pick up as you go along, making adjustments as you learn more about your body and what type of fueling it responds well to. After a while you won't even need to track your eating, because you will have developed good habits. And that's the key to sustainable weight loss. A diet built around deprivation, or based on expensive meal replacement shakes and bars won't last. Either your willpower will crumble, or once you go back to eating regular food you will gain weight again because you've learned nothing about healthy eating.

I won't tell you that you have to follow a specific system. I've tried vegetarianism, Paleo, no-carb, no sugar, and many other variations. But what I've settled on, and what works for me today, is a lifestyle that cuts out most processed foods and is based on food we prepare ourselves from simple ingredients. I don't even track calories or macros at this point. If I eat right, I have energy to get through the day, and I don't gain weight. If I eat badly, I'll notice immediately. Fatigue, headaches, moodiness, stomach problems, gas and bloating. Any of those things are a sign that I've let something unhealthy into my eating. When you consistently eat healthy over a sustained period of time, you realize just how bad all that other food was for you. Suddenly the free pizzas for staying late to work on a project are a lot less appealing.

Here's an example of a typical day of food for me now if you're looking for ideas:

- **Breakfast** is a glass of water straight away, then a coffee with a dash of milk and a breakfast burrito. I make a batch of burritos each week. Some are bacon and egg, and the others are chicken or turkey with black beans, corn, and a little salsa and cheese for flavor. They freeze easily, and it's just a matter of defrosting them overnight and toasting them up in the sandwich press for a few minutes. My kids love them too. They haven't eaten packaged breakfast cereal in a long time.

- I exercise early in the day before work starts, so depending on what my workout was I'll have a smoothie for a **mid-morning snack** with some coconut water, half a frozen banana, berries, and some protein (hemp protein powder is my current favorite). If you don't have access to a blender, get your hands on a protein shaker and just eat the fruit along with it.

- **Lunch** will be leftovers from dinner, or a simple salad with some protein added, and some carbs like brown rice. My wife cooks a whole chicken on the weekend, so there's always shredded chicken ready to add to salads and wraps.

- With my **afternoon coffee** (although I'm trying to switch to tea instead) I'll have a little snack, such as a date and almond energy ball that I make at home each week, or apple slices with some almond butter.

- **Dinner** will depend on the day of the week. We have a mixed routine during the week. Some nights there's time to cook a whole meal, other times we're taking the kids to after school activities and events and we rely on slow cooker meals or prepped meals that just need reheating. As an example, tonight we had a simple Thai beef stir fry. No processed, sugary stir fry sauces involved. Just fresh ingredients, a little soy sauce, some basil, and some brown rice to go with it. Each weekend we also try one new recipe that we've found online, and if we like it then we add it to the rotation.

- Throw in a piece of fruit or some coconut yoghurt for **dessert** if necessary.

And that's it. All of that food is delicious and healthy. I have consistent energy all day without the sugar spikes and crashes that a diet high in processed carbs and sugar causes. Better energy means better focus, which improves the quality of my work. Producing quality work provides a feeling of satisfaction and fulfillment, which in turn helps to maintain happiness. And being happy in our daily lives is the goal here.

There's no need to punish yourself with low calorie diets, or strictly exclude certain foods. Deprivation just leads to resentment and unhappiness. We never feel deprived or bored with the food we eat. There's still the occasional restaurant meal or treat thrown into the mix, but even at restaurants we tend to choose healthier options. If you build a lifestyle around healthy food that tastes good, I know that you will start to look and feel a lot healthier.

Tips for Healthy Eating

It's not easy to change from an unhealthy diet of packaged, processed foods to a healthy lifestyle all in one go. Here are some tips to help you make the transition.

» Solve one problem at a time. Pick one thing, such as snacks or breakfast, and focus on changing that in the first week. When you have that under control, move on to lunch, then dinner.

» Try one new healthy recipe each week. We find that weekends are perfect for this because there is more time to go shopping for fresh ingredients that we don't already have at home, and slowly work through an unfamiliar recipe.

» Save time and avoid decision fatigue by meal planning and prepping. Instead of worrying each day what you're going to eat, plan out your entire week's meals and do some meal prep on the weekends to get ready for them. We make batches of snacks, lunches that can be frozen and reheated, and even dinners for nights that we know we'll be home late with little time to cook.

» Cook extra portions for dinner as well, and freeze those for lunches and emergency dinners later.

» Track your calories with an app like MyFitnessPal, at least for a few weeks while you learn what works and what doesn't. In the long term your goal should be to have a healthy lifestyle that runs on autopilot without constant tracking. If you feel like you're starting to slip a bit, start tracking again for a week or two and make the necessary adjustments.

» If you're trying to eat healthy and you're constantly hungry it means you're eating too much of the wrong things, or not enough of the right things. Eating healthy doesn't mean starving yourself.

EXERCISE

Good nutrition is the foundation of a healthy life. But exercise plays an important part as well. For people who are trying to lose some weight like I was, exercise is a key part of burning off more energy than you consume in a day.

My gym membership and personal trainer got me started on my fitness journey. But getting fit in the gym with no other goal in mind is not how I personally am able to maintain motivation. Sure, for a while it was enough to set goals such as improving my bench press or deadlift. But I needed more than that.

The two changes that provided the biggest motivation boosts for me to continue exercising were:

1. Exercising as a means of transport
2. Exercising as a social activity

Making exercise a form of transportation was fairly simple for me. I'm fortunate to live in a part of the world where the depths of winter involve wearing a coat for three to four weeks. For the rest of the year, the morning and evening temperatures are mild enough for outdoor activities. We also have bike paths on many of the main roads that run in and out of the city, and most suburban areas are pretty safe for cyclists as well. I happened to be working in a building with shower and locker facilities, so after a few chats to my colleagues I decided to stop taking the train to and from work and take up cycling instead.

A decent bicycle and accessories cost about the same as a year of train trips, so financially it was an easy decision. Logistically it took a few weeks to adjust. I had to store my work clothes in my locker at the office, and started using a dry cleaner near work to clean them. That just left my lunch and a clean pair of socks to carry in my backpack while I was cycling.

Physically the rides were brutal to begin with. Cycling uses different muscles than weight lifting and running. But my body adjusted quickly and before long I was cruising in and out of the city each day on my bike, getting a decent workout each time.

Exercising as a social activity took a little bit more effort. Since I love basketball I decided to put my name down at the local club to see if I could get onto a team. I got a call within a few weeks, but ended up on a team that was pretty hopeless. I'm no superstar myself though, and I'm only average height. So I just treated each game as a good excuse to get out and run around, meet people, and have a few laughs. We won maybe two or three games that year.

These days I have retired from basketball and am an avid trail runner. Running trails is a very social activity. I can run alone, or with a friend, or with one of many running groups in this area that organize group runs on Facebook.

Exercise has a funny way of adjusting your nutritional intake for you. Once you're hooked on running, you start to push your limits and try to see how much further or faster you can run. The more you run, the more aware you become of how your body responds to the fuel you give it. Eating a diet of processed food results in poor performance. Eating a diet of clean, healthy foods will have you running further than you ever thought possible.

Exercise is also great for your mental health. I've lost count of the number of big, complex problems I've solved in my mind while out for a run. And even a quick jog at lunchtime is enough to remove the morning's stress and set me up for a more relaxed, productive afternoon.

Tips for Fitting Exercise Into Your Day

The most important thing with exercise is to make time for it. Don't wait until you can find time. I know not everyone can get to the gym in the morning or evenings, so here are some tips on other ways you can fit exercise into your busy day.

» Join a sports club or cycling/running/walking group to make exercise a social event.

» Add exercise to your normal routine. Get off the bus or train one stop earlier, and walk the rest of the way to the office. Or turn your whole commute into a workout by running or cycling to work.

» Use your lunch break for exercising. If you have a nearby gym, it's possible to walk there, get changed, do a 30-minute intense workout, shower and dress, and be back at your desk within the hour. Eat your lunch afterwards while you work.

» To save even more time at the gym, ask your boss if you can take lunch earlier to avoid peak times at the gym.

» If your office has showers and change facilities, put on some running clothes and shoes and take a nice easy jog for 30 minutes during your lunch break.

» If the weather is bad, find a place to exercise in your building. Try a bodyweight workout routine in the basement carpark. Or just put on some music or podcasts and walk up and down the internal stairs.

» Not all workouts need to be intense. Change things up by adding in yoga or a good stretching session. There are lots of routines available for free on YouTube that you can follow along with.

DRUGS AND ALCOHOL

Here in Australia the legal age for drinking alcohol is 18. So, by the time most people leave high school, complete some tertiary education, and enter a professional career, they are already old enough to drink.

When I started my first IT job I had no money, and a lot of debt. I was also living in a new city, so I didn't have any friends yet. That kept me away from the after-work social scene for quite a while. Eventually I started to get my finances under control, and a beer or two after work became a regular event. I worked in the city, so leaving the office on a Friday night and heading to a bar was pretty easy to do. Naturally that grew into a regular Friday night drinking session with the same people.

About 18 months into my first job I was offered the chance to move to Sydney to work on a project. I decided to accept the role, packed up my belongings, and moved into a room at a house I shared with two other guys that I'd never met. They were friendly, but had their own separate social lives, and were never around on weekends. I realized pretty quickly that the reason for that was there was nothing to do on weekends near our house. I had chosen the location because it was easy to get to the office every day. I hadn't thought about whether there were fun things to do nearby on my down time.

Not that it mattered. The project I was working on was not very challenging, and I was working less than 40 hours most weeks. I was enjoying the quiet time, and had taken up running as a hobby. With no Friday night drinking to recover from, I suddenly had a lot more time and energy on weekends. I settled into a routine of coming home from work each day, going for a run, cooking a simple meal, and then watching a movie or playing some games. On weekends I would run some more, do my laundry and other tasks, study a little, watch more movies, and play more games. I lost a heap of weight, felt healthy and energetic, and aside from a little boredom now and then, was generally feeling pretty good.

That continued for six months until the project finished and I moved back to Brisbane and my old job again. That meant returning to the same social scene, so of course I started going out on Friday nights again. Pretty soon I was back to my old habits. My health started to decline, though I didn't notice at the time.

Fast forward a few years, and I was working in a pretty high stress role for a managed service provider. One day I took stock of my situation and realized something. Like the rest of the team, I worked under a lot of pressure during the week. By Friday afternoon everyone was strung out and exhausted. Then the drinks fridge would be unlocked, and everyone would let the stress out by drinking heavily for an hour or two before heading home. Some of us kept drinking and would head out into the city to continue.

I found myself in a weekly cycle of being stressed to breaking point, and then using alcohol as a release valve to let it all out. I wasn't drinking because I wanted to, I was drinking because I felt like I had to. This didn't sit well with me, and one Saturday morning as I literally looked at myself in the mirror, I didn't like what I saw.

Overweight, bags under my red eyes, pale skin. I looked terrible and was spending every weekend recovering from my big Friday night out. I wasn't studying or learning anything new. I was really going nowhere at all.

If this was a perfect story I would tell you that I turned my life around at that point. But that's not what happened at all. Instead, I tried to go one month without drinking any alcohol. It was hard, especially on that first Friday afternoon when all my colleagues were opening their first beer. I had a Diet Coke instead. I got through those four weeks without drinking. And then I started drinking again.

It wasn't until a few years later that I worked out a better solution that balanced my enjoyment of drinking (I have a small whiskey collection, and enjoy good beers), with my desire to not use alcohol as a means to offset to the stress and pressure of work.

I attacked the problem in two ways. The first was to reduce the stress and pressure that work created. Earlier in this chapter I wrote about life-work balance, and the need to fight for good working conditions that don't have you constantly overworked and under pressure. I fought that fight for years, slowly improving my situation through a combination of standing up for myself, and finding employers who treat their employees well.

The second method that I used was to adopt a simple rule. I would no longer get drunk in front of customers. As a consultant or project engineer I felt it was important to maintain a good, professional relationship with customers. Getting drunk in front of them would undermine that. Seeing the customers drunk would also undermine it. It was acceptable for me to have a beer or two with customers, but I always left before the event started to get a bit loose.

Working for internal IT departments was a bit more of a challenge. Going to the company Christmas party would mean being surrounded by colleagues who were actually your customers. So again, no drinking. In fact, I found it easier to either skip the party, or volunteer to cover for my team and keep an eye on our systems so they could attend the party if it was being held during business hours.

Once I had the work-related drinking under control, I started to look at ways to deal with social drinking. I'm not uncomfortable drinking around my friends and family, but I have made my health a priority in my life now. So I have a rule for that as well. I can drink as much as I want to, but I still have to get up the next day and exercise. That keeps me from blowing out and having a big night, most of the time. I'm not perfect, and I still slip up. But one of the things I'm proud of in my journey to better health is waking up the day after my 40th birthday celebrations and still managing to get a 4km (almost 2.5 miles) run done at my normal pace. That is a far cry from the old me who would have spent three to four days recovering from the party.

Why am I telling you all of this? It's simple. I don't want to dictate to you whether or not you should be drinking or taking drugs (legal or otherwise). You're a grown up, it's your life, and that's your personal decision to make. As long as you can show up to work and do your job well then that will keep most employers satisfied.

What I'm suggesting, and what I'm trying to get across from sharing my personal story, is that you should look at your habits and ask yourself whether they're holding you back from achieving your goals, growing your career into what you want it to be, and living your best life.

Say you've been meaning to lose weight, maybe you joined a gym and started bringing your lunch from home. But if you're then drinking on weekends, and eating lots of 'drunk food' or 'hangover food,' you're undoing all that good work during the week.

If you've been meaning to learn to code, maybe you have your eye on a training course to follow. But then if you're spending your free time out partying, and you're too tired and hungover to sit down and do the training, you're not learning much at all.

If you want that promotion, but you spend half the week recovering from all the partying you did on the weekend, then you're not going to be performing at a high enough level to impress the powers that be.

Decide what's important in your life. Then give the important things in your life the priority they deserve.

CHAPTER 6 RECAP

- Poor life-work balance, negative attitude, declining mental health and declining physical health are all signs of burnout. Be alert to them because making changes *before* a total breakdown is easier than making changes *after* a total breakdown.

- Don't aim for work-life balance, aim for life-work balance. Having a life is crucial to avoiding burnout and maintaining your health and happiness.

- Sound physical health is underpinned by a healthy approach to eating, a commitment to regular exercise, and consuming alcohol in moderation. You need to find sustainable approaches to all these things otherwise you won't be able to maintain them long-term.

CHAPTER 7
VETERAN ADVICE

When you've been in an industry for more than 20 years, you build up a fair bank of things you wish you'd known when you first started in that industry. This chapter covers off items that weren't worthy of an entire chapter, but that I consider to be 'savvy veteran advice' that can stop you making some of the mistakes I did in the early days.

HOW TO BE WRONG

The best time to admit you're wrong is as soon as you realize that you are wrong. Digging in your heels and escalating a debate when you know you're wrong is bad for your professional reputation, for your team's harmony, and for people's opinion of you.

The key to graceful acceptance of being wrong is to always keep your mind open to the possibility that you are wrong. There is so much scope for knowledge gaps in the IT profession, this should always be a possibility in your mind. Technology is complex. Even when technology is well-understood, the way technology is implemented can leave gaps in your understanding of how something works.

By keeping an open mind, you can have calm and respectful discussions about a problem without painting yourself into a corner. Avoid using inflammatory language that makes you and the other parties want to double down on your opinions. Keep things friendly and non-threatening by using phrases such as "My understanding of that is ..." and "In the past when I've seen this happen, it has been ...."

When you learn new facts that make you realize you're wrong, you can genuinely thank the other person without feeling like they have won some sort of intellectual victory over you. Use phrases such as "I was never sure exactly how that fit together, thank you for clearing that up."

It's also good to remember that being wrong is a natural part of your daily work in finding the right answers to problems. When investigating problems you will have to go through a process of elimination. Of the ten possible solutions to a problem, the faster you can identify the nine that are wrong, the sooner you will arrive at the solution that is correct.

So get used to being wrong. And build a reputation of admitting when you are wrong. Nobody will keep score. Quite the contrary. Most people would prefer to work with someone open-minded and willing to accept their own knowledge gaps.

TECHNICAL DEBT

Technical debt is the cost, usually measured in time, of additional rework that accumulates when you choose an easy solution to a problem instead of a better solution that would take longer to implement. In other words, the time you save today is a debt that needs to be repaid in the future.

Sometimes technical debt is necessary and desirable. Today's 'quick fix' may be important to restore service to a critical business system. The problem is when the quick fix becomes the permanent solution. Like a bad loan with a high interest rate, technical debt tends to grow if not paid off quickly.

Technical debt adds constraints to future work. If you want to make a change in the future, but first you need to do the rework on your previously implemented easy fixes, it makes it harder to find the time and resources to make the new change. Eventually, you start to feel like it's impossible to get anything done at all due to decisions made in the past. Some of those decisions will be yours. Some will have been made by your superiors, or your predecessors, and were out of your control. You might even resent them for making those decisions, even though they may have been necessary due to constraints at the time.

The first solution for technical debt is to quit your job. This is the easy solution. You get to walk away from the problems and get a fresh start at a new job. Or at least, that's how it seems. There is a risk that your new job will be saddled with even more technical debt than your last job. That won't be immediately obvious. Technical debt tends to reveal itself slowly as you work in a new environment and try to make changes and improvements. And if the employees who made the decisions that caused that technical debt are not still working there, you'll have limited information about what problems and constraints led to that situation in the first place.

Quitting also robs you of the opportunity to gain new skills by solving the problems that are in front of you. This is the second solution, to stay and pay down the technical debt. Naturally, it is also the harder solution.

Paying off technical debt is only partly dependent on your technical skills. There is a far greater dependency on your ability to break down complex work into manageable chunks, make convincing business cases to invest in long term solutions, and use time management skills to get the work done.

Quitting might seem like the logical choice for someone who values a healthy life-work balance. Why work hard to solve problems that someone else created? I don't believe in that point of view myself. In fact, I believe that staying and solving technical debt problems can provide you with a better life-work balance in the long term. The possible benefits include:

- Proving your value to your current employer, and using that to build a case for the role you want (e.g. a promotion, a pay raise, or switch to remote work).

- Building better, more resilient systems that require less maintenance and after hours work.

- The stories and experience you accumulate that will be highly valuable in any future job interviews.

- Extra money, if the employer is willing to pay you overtime for the extra project work.

Of course, none of those are guarantees. You are always taking a risk to stay in a job and and solve technical debt problems. If you are convinced that nothing will change, that you won't make any progress, and all you'll be doing is wasting your time, then perhaps it is time to move on after all.

ADDICTION TO FIREFIGHTING

Wikipedia defines 'hero syndrome' as a phenomenon affecting people who seek heroism or recognition, usually by creating a desperate situation which they can resolve.

It's a nice feeling when you save the day. Some of my strongest memories throughout my career are of major events where I and my team battled a critical systems failure and restored service.

But have you ever seen those people who seem to rush from one emergency to the next? Everything is a disaster that needs an immediate response. Every solution is a release of pressure, until the next emergency appears not long after.

Like the firefighter who dabbles in arson on the side, those people are addicted to solving crises.

But constant firefighting is exhausting work. And it gets you nowhere. All you're doing is beating back the flames and returning the status quo. Nothing ever really gets better. Which suits some people just fine. If you can fill up your day fighting fires, you're under no pressure to fill time with meaningful work that helps the business to grow and prosper.

At some point the customer is going to wise up. Why do we keep having so many problems? Why isn't there any improvement?

I'm going to level with you, there are only two reasons that IT systems run in a constant state of emergency:

1. The business isn't investing in good systems.
2. The IT department or provider is failing the business.

If you work for a business that doesn't take IT seriously, there's probably not much you can do. Find solutions, design upgrades and improvements, ask for the money to make them happen. Connect them to metrics that the business cares about. Be lean and economical. Stretch budgets as far as they will go. And if they still say no, you get to choose whether to stay on and fight fires for a living, or leave.

YOU'RE NOT A MAGICIAN

Here's a list of things you can't do:

- be in two places at once
- travel long distances at a moment's notice
- read your email while you're asleep
- work without sleeping at all
- instantly conjure up replacement hardware

- know the precise time that a broken thing will be fixed

- travel back in time

- explain events that you did not witness

- find every bug in every piece of third party software you run

- read minds

- hit a moving target

- fit 80 hours of work into 40 hours

- make the internet go faster

- reconstruct lost data using hope and tears

- never take a day off

While an employer would never expressly ask you to do any of the above, they may make requests of you that require the above things to be within the realm of reality. If you're not able to communicate with your employer that their expectations are unreasonable and indeed, unachievable, it might be time to find a new employer.

SUCCESS AS A BARRIER TO SUCCESS

When you do a task well, your boss will give you more of that task to do. This can be both a blessing and a curse.

If you demonstrate a knack for pulling out-of-control projects back from the brink of disaster, you'll be the one they call every time a project is about to blow up. If you demonstrate a skill for coding reliable scripts for automating processes, you'll be asked to write more code to automate more processes. If you've got good personal skills and a knack for making customers happy, you'll be the one sent in to placate every angry customer.

If you enjoy the task, then you'll be happy to do more if it. I happen to enjoy writing scripts, so being given the task to automate a process is enjoyable for me. On the other hand, even though I've saved a few projects from becoming disasters, it's not an experience that I'd like to repeat. I'd rather be involved in projects right from the start, instead of only stepping in when they are falling apart.

In the short term, working on tasks that you're good at, but that you don't enjoy, is not especially harmful to your career. In fact, I recommend you happily accept work that you're not highly interested in, but are capable of doing well. It's part of being a good team player. But over the years it can steer your career in directions that you don't necessarily want to go. One day, you might just realize that you don't like anything about your job, even though you're good at it.

I see this quite a lot. IT professionals find themselves in a position where they can't understand why they don't like the job that they're doing, even though they still feel that interest in technology in general. It's a confusing situation if you don't recognize it for what it is.

The further you get from your ideal job, the harder it is to make a switch. If you've been successful at doing the things you're good at, then you're probably getting paid a good salary to do it. Taking a pay cut to move into a different area of IT that you're more interested in is a difficult decision to make. Especially if you have debt, or a family that depends on your income.

Obviously the ideal solution is to avoid the problem in the first place. Or at least recognize when you're in the situation, and start to plan a way out of it. If you find yourself repeatedly doing the same tasks, ask yourself whether you can see yourself doing that same task every day. Consider whether the job you're doing has you positioned where you want to be on the technology adoption curve (see Chapter 1).

If you find yourself heading in a direction that you don't want to go, then you have two options:

1. **Talk to your boss about aligning your role with your interests.** This will involve some give and take on your part. It may be that you're being asked to do something that nobody else on the team can do. Before you can stop doing that task, you need to make it possible for others to do it. That could mean writing documentation, delivering training, or improving a system to avoid that problem happening in the first place. In most cases, if you're willing to invest some effort into solving the problem, then your boss will be open to change.

2. **Find another job.** Use the opportunity in job interviews to discover if a prospective employer has the same problems you're trying to escape. If poor project management or resourcing is the problem, ask the interviewers about how they manage their projects. How do they staff their project teams? How often do projects run over schedule? What project management methodologies do they use? Look up their current and former project managers on LinkedIn to see how long they've been with the company.

What if you can't change your job or find a new one? Maybe you live in an area where there are very few jobs available. Moving your entire life to another place is a big step. I couldn't imagine uprooting my whole family, forcing my wife to change jobs and my kids to change schools, just because I was unhappy with my job.

This is where a focus on life-work balance and happiness outside of work, both of which are core messages of this book, will help you to get through the boring, uncomfortable, or just plain bad jobs during your career.

COMFORT IS THE ENEMY OF PROGRESS

When you get good at something you start to feel very comfortable doing it. Whether it's a scripting language, a development framework, or a specific tool, being good at it feels good.

When we're comfortable, we like to stop and enjoy it for a while. Like sitting on the couch after a long day, and not wanting to get up and cook dinner. We want to stop and relax. Everything else can wait.

But technology doesn't stop. Things keep moving while we're sitting there enjoying the comfort. Along comes something new and different from what we're comfortable with. People say it's better. But there's a learning curve. Learning new things is uncomfortable, and sitting still is very comfortable. So comfort wins.

The trouble is, while you sit there in your comfort,

other people keep moving. The longer you wait, the further they move ahead of you. Now it's no longer uncomfortable to learn something new, it's a frantic race to catch up. Because getting left behind in the technology industry spells career death.

Comfort is the enemy of progress. And if you aren't moving forward, you're moving backwards.

Enjoy your growth as a professional and a person. Enjoy what you've learned. Enjoy the feeling of accomplishment, of being skilled and capable. Then build on it. Don't sit in comfort. Continue to make progress.

How do we do that? Commit to learning and expanding your knowledge. Read one interesting article or blog post each day. I use a variety of resources to help with this:

- I use Feedly and a bunch of RSS feeds to keep up with what's happening in my areas of interest. Almost every day a great article appears in one of those feeds that teaches me something I didn't know before. I skim through the feeds in the morning, and add anything interesting to Pocket to read at lunch or after dinner.

- I scan Medium every few days for interesting articles. Like anything, Medium has its fair share of content that isn't of use to me personally. But at least once a week I'll find a great article on technology, or productivity, or personal growth.

- I subscribe to a series of curated newsletters. I'm interested in Python programming, so I've subscribed to the Python Weekly newsletter. As a beginner, a lot of it goes over my head. But I also find interesting, beginner-friendly articles to read.

- I'm a paid supporter of Longreads. At least once a week I find an amazing long form article worth sitting down to read with a coffee on a Saturday morning.

- I often listen to audiobooks and podcasts when I'm running, doing tasks around the house, or cooking.

I recommend you also set aside the time to do two to four hours of focussed learning each week. Block it out in your personal calendar, so you always know it's there and you aren't tempted to fill that time with other things.

You don't need to study and cram every single day and night. In fact, I recommend you don't. I don't always do this. Sometimes it's better to do something in silence and let your brain process a problem or some knowledge you've already exposed it to that day. Rest and idle time are as important to learning as the actual learning itself.

Rewards are also important. Operating in a permanent state of deprivation is exhausting, and builds up resentment. I find it hard to forgo playing my PS4 to sit down and study every single night. But I find it much easier to say, "Thursday night is my study night, and if I get it done then I can play games on Friday night."

Each month take stock of what you've learned. If you haven't learned anything new, ask yourself why. Did you get 'too busy'? Nobody is too busy for one article a day and a couple hours a week of learning.

It's a matter of priorities, and not letting yourself sit in comfort all the time.

DON'T TAKE THINGS PERSONALLY

"We've decided not to proceed."

Those five words opened the meeting, and I took a moment to compose myself. I'd just been told that a solution I had worked on for a year was getting scrapped.

It wasn't just my solution. A team of us had worked together to try and get it happening. The idea was bold. Implementing a backup solution that would address a customer's concerns about data restoration times in a large email environment. It was a lot of data, in a complex environment, with a limited budget to make it work. You might think it was an impossible task. We gave it our best shot anyway.

After a year of design work, testing, problems, troubleshooting, and vendor support calls, we actually got it working. The problem was, it was going to cost a lot of money to run it. So the customer decided to cancel the project. They dropped the news to us in a project meeting on a Friday afternoon.

In my younger days this type of situation would upset me. All my hard work flushed down the drain by some upper level manager who didn't understand the technical side of things. I'd spend time and energy complaining to my peers, then waste even more time and energy sitting in quiet frustration.

But this time I didn't get upset. After more than a decade of seeing projects succeed and fail, I'd stopped taking these things personally. For one thing, it doesn't help the situation. My energy is a finite resource. Spending it on something that can't be changed is pointless. And being a serial complainer, someone who whines when things don't go their way, isn't a label I want to earn for myself.

Just because an idea is good, that doesn't mean it deserves to be implemented. Some ideas don't fit the situation. Sometimes a different idea is chosen, even if your idea was better. There are any number of reasons why that can happen, including political reasons. When there's room for just one idea to be chosen, yours won't always be the one. If it's a good idea it will get another chance in the future.

The solution can be elegant and efficient, but that doesn't mean it solves a big enough problem to earn a place in the environment. Maybe another solution is simpler. Maybe another solution is more complex and impressive sounding. And maybe the best solution is to just do nothing at all.

Your sales proposal can hit all the right points, but that doesn't mean the customer can't choose someone else. It happens. Another customer will come along.

If a customer doesn't like you, why would you want to work with them? You wouldn't. And if it's something you can change, whether it be your hair, your clothes, the way you present your ideas, the price you charge, then you can decide whether to change or not. If you like the way you are, accept the customers who don't see you as a fit, and seek to please the customers who think you're the right fit.

It's hardly ever personal. And even when it is, you shouldn't take it personally. Your ideas can live on and find new life when the next opportunity comes along, if you let them.

CHAPTER 7 RECAP

- When you're willing to be wrong, and admit you're wrong when you are, it is good for your professional reputation, for your team's harmony, and for people's opinion of you.

- As frustrating as it can be, technical debt offers the opportunity to gain new skills by solving the problems that are in front of you. These skills will stand you in good stead in future salary negotiations with your current employer, or help you secure a role with a new employer.

- Let go of your addiction to firefighting. It gets in the way of doing meaningful work that helps your business grow and prosper.

- If your employer is sending you subtle messages that they expect you to be able to do the impossible, either address these unrealistic expectations with them, or find a new employer.

- Beware of the curse of competence. You might quickly find yourself spending your days doing things you're good at, but don't especially enjoy.

- Beware of getting too comfortable. A simple program of continued learning and growth need not be onerous or time consuming. And will ensure you never find yourself left behind.

- Don't take business decisions personally. A large number of factors come into play when these decisions are being made, seldom are those factors personal to you, and choosing to depersonalize those decisions will significantly benefit your mental health.

CONCLUSION

Remember the perfect day you outlined for yourself at the start of this book? I'm not going to promise you that you will achieve it right away. It might take you several years to get close, as it has for me. Or, it might take you just a few changes in your life to get there. But you'll never get close if you don't know what you're aiming for.

I recently ran my first ultramarathon, a 50km (31 miles) trail race through the iconic Blue Mountains of New South Wales. Finishing an ultramarathon is a long way from the overweight, unhappy, stressed out person that woke up in the middle of the night with chest pains. That guy all those years ago was more concerned with not dying. Today, I'm only concerned with what fun thing I'm going to do next in my life.

Because I chose to take on an ultramarathon as a life goal, I had to sit down and think very carefully about how to approach it. Traveling that distance on foot is not something that happens by accident. If I'd shown up on race day untrained and unprepared I would have dropped out of the race early, been pulled from the race for missing a cutoff time, or (most likely) injured myself.

There wasn't one big thing I had to change to make the day a success. Instead, I had to make a number of small changes to my diet, sleep habits, training regime, clothing, and equipment over a period of time. It wasn't easy to make all those changes. And I didn't get them right on the first attempt. Even the simple question of what to eat and drink during the race to keep me fueled took a lot of research and testing.

To achieve my goal of completing an ultramarathon I knew I would need to approach it the right way. I expanded my personal network by joining local and online running groups. I took advice from others who have experience running that race and others like it. I learned a lot from them, not only in the answers to my own questions, but also the questions that others asked that I hadn't thought of. People I met within those groups have become friends, and we've helped motivate each other by meeting up for training runs together. Nothing like a bit of mutual obligation to get you out of bed on a cold morning.

Just like staying up to date with technology, I needed to understand the products in the trail and ultra running industry. I tested food, hydration, shoes, vests, and clothing—right down to knowing the exact pair of socks that would let me run long distances without blisters. For each of them I went through the same process. What problems do they solve? What types of runners use them? Do they meet one of my own needs?

I can tinker around and learn a few things on my own, but I learn best by following structured training content. So I purchased an ultramarathon training plan that was written specifically for this race and came highly recommended. I mapped out the six months leading up to race day and committed myself to doing one thing each day to get me to that goal. Every day I got up early for a training run, did stretching and foam rolling, or did a gym workout. I was diligent about my training days, but also about my rest days, prioritizing sleep and relaxation as often as necessary to keep me feeling fresh and motivated. Overtraining leads to burnout and injury, which caused a lot of aspiring runners to have to drop out and sell their ticket before race day.

I gave my race preparations the exact priority level in my life they deserved. Above most things, but below the most important things like my family. On one memorable morning I woke up at 2:30am so that I could set off on a five hour training run and still finish in time to make it to my son's basketball game.

I eliminated the unnecessary things in life that didn't move me towards my goal, but kept enough space to allow some things in from time to time. I still went to parties, a few nights out with friends, had a few beers now and then, watched some TV, and enjoyed life in general. But I didn't waste time on anything that kept me away from my training.

It's hard to just put your head down and slog away at a goal for months on end. We need to see progress to remind ourselves how far we've come, and refresh our energy and motivation. So I ran a few other local races during my training to measure my progress. Each one gave me the opportunity to test out my pre-race routines, test my pacing strategies, try out a piece of gear or a nutrition plan, and make some other adjustments.

As race day approached I used the same strategies as I use for job interviews to plan out my logistics. Where will we stay? Where can we buy food so I have a good pre-race meal? How do we get to the race precinct on the day? What time will we need to wake up, and what time will we need to be out the door so that I make my start time?

Race day was like a mini version of my ideal day. It had moments of hard work, but also fun and happiness. My family was there to support me. I was doing something I loved, surrounded by like minded people that I enjoyed being with. If I could get paid to do it, it would have been perfect.

When I crossed the finish line and hugged my wife and kids it was one of the most satisfying moments of my life. I'd achieved my goal of running an ultramarathon. I felt like I'd given it my all, and left nothing in reserve. The time wasn't important to me. It didn't matter to me that hundreds of people beat me, or that I beat hundreds of other people. Finishing was what I set out to achieve.

I allowed myself to enjoy the moment, and enjoy the pay off as well. A few sleep ins, eating some treat meals, and playing more video games in a weekend than I'd played the whole month prior. Within a week I was thinking about the next goals that would add purpose to my life, and starting the mental exercise of planning how they would fit in.

Setting a goal, consistently working to achieve it, and then seeing the results is a feeling that stays with you forever. Achieving the same in your career creates a feeling of happiness and fulfillment on a daily basis. And I believe that any of us, including you, can achieve this.

So where do you begin?

Asking yourself, "What does my perfect day look like?" is a good start. Take a few minutes, if you haven't already, to think about that question and write down some ideas. Keep tweaking it until you've got a nice, clear image of what your perfect day would be. Use that ideal day as the goal that inspires you to keep moving forward.

- Decide where you want to be in the technology industry. An innovator? An early adopter? A late adopter? This will determine many things, including which technologies you should focus on, which job markets have the opportunities in those areas, and what type of companies you should pursue working for.

- Examine the jobs in those areas. What skills do they ask for? What gaps do you need to fill to position yourself for those roles? Are you already a decent candidate? Don't reject yourself, start applying right away. You might get lucky and land a job quickly. If not, you'll at least have made a start on refining your application and interview skills.

- Expand your personal network. What meetups and online communities can you get involved in to learn from others, grow your skills, and contribute as well?

- Create something noteworthy. Start a project or blog that showcases your skills and builds your reputation. It doesn't need to be huge. A useful script or tool, some code samples, a curated newsletter, or a once-weekly blog is all it takes.

- Work on your personal skills. Push yourself outside your comfort zone. Pick up hobbies that involve other people, and that give you things to talk about in conversation with others. Read books and arm yourself with the simple techniques that can get you through any social or professional situation.

- Make better use of your time. Ditch time-wasting activities that add no value to your day. Learn new habits that make the best use of your time, allow you to do quality work, and leave enough space in your day to study, pursue hobbies, and spend time with loved ones.

- Prioritize your health. Establish boundaries at your job and stop working excessive hours. Take up healthy hobbies that involve physical activity. Learn to prepare and cook simple, healthy meals. Stop relying on caffeine and other substances to deal with stress. Establish more discipline in the evenings so that you go to bed and get enough sleep each night.

You should end up with a list of changes that will move you closer to your ideal day. If the changes are big ones, such as changing jobs or relocating to a new city, break them down further into what steps are necessary to make them happen. If you have a partner or family, discuss your goals and plans with them too, because any changes you make will also impact their lives.

It doesn't need to be a huge overhaul all at once. Just commit to doing one thing each day, or changing one thing each week that will move you towards your ideal day. Pick one problem, and solve that first. If you're not sure where to start, the top three changes that most people need to make are:

1. Stop working excessive hours
2. Get more sleep
3. Eat healthier

In just a few weeks you'll feel less stressed and more energized, giving you a solid foundation to keep making changes in other areas.

Treat your life like a marathon, not a sprint. Find the right pace that keeps you moving without crashing in a heap. Take that first step. Then take another. And don't stop until you reach the finish line.

THANK YOU

Thanks so much for reading. If you've found Surviving IT helpful I'd love to get your feedback. You can email **paul@survivingitbook.com** to let me know your thoughts.

I'd also appreciate you helping spread the word by leaving a review on Amazon.

CPSIA information can be obtained
at www.ICGtesting.com
Printed in the USA
BVHW080903120919
558269BV00015B/1647/P